FINDING THE HISTORICAL JESUS

FINDING
THE HISTORICAL
JESUS

A STATEMENT OF THE
PRINCIPLES INVOLVED

by

JAMES PETER

HARPER & ROW, PUBLISHERS, NEW YORK

Contents

CONTENTS

The dawn that arose in Palestine has still to unfold its greater splendours, and the historian has his own necessary part in the dissipating of the shadows.

Amos N. Wilder, *Otherworldliness and the New Testament, p.* 43

Introduction

THE QUEST of the historical Jesus did not begin with
Reimarus and it did not end with Wrede.[1] Always
there have been those to maintain that, however much
else Christian faith may involve, it cannot avoid some
estimate of Jesus himself.

Any attempt at such an estimate is an attempt at
finding the historical Jesus. And, since such attempts
are always being made, it is important that the principles governing them be understood.

Christianity is frequently referred to as a historical
religion—a statement which rests upon such varied
factors as the Gospel writers' attempts to fix certain
happenings by reference to persons and events outside
the main stream of their narrative,[2] the credal declaration, "suffered under Pontius Pilate", and the assertions made by many Christians over the centuries.

John Macquarrie[3] is right to draw attention to the
fact that not all who advance the claim that Christianity
is a historical religion make obvious what they mean

[1]*Von Reimarus zu Wrede* was the original title of *The Quest of the Historical Jesus* by Albert Schweitzer. The position advanced there is
discussed in chapter I.
[2]e.g. Matthew 2.1; 14.1; Mark 6.14; Luke 2.1-3; 3.1-2; 9.7;
13.1; 23.8; John 18.13.
[3]John Macquarrie, *The Scope of Demythologizing* (New York:

by it. An eminent contemporary historian, however, has pointed out that Christianity is a historical religion in a particular technical sense of that phrase: "It presents us with religious doctrines which are at the same time historical events or historical interpretations."[4] He says again: "Certain historical events are held to be part of the religion itself—they are considered to have a spiritual content and to represent the divine breaking in upon history."[5]

Here there is clarification of what the claim means, and also of where the problem lies. Certain events are "historical" *and* "represent the divine breaking in upon history." It is not clear how both these statements can be true.

We can put this in concrete terms. If the life of Jesus is coincident with the lives of other men, it must be possible to examine that life in the same way as other lives in the past can be examined. Since, however, it is maintained by Christians at the same time that the person who lived this life is somehow different from all other men, it seems to be implied that this life cannot be examined just as other men's can.

This is the core of the problem of Jesus to-day. What relationship, if any, is there between the figure known and open to historiographical investigation and the figure acknowledged by Christians as the supreme revelation of God? In other words, how is the historian's Jesus related to the believer's Jesus?[6] Stated in

---

Harper & Row, 1960), p. 58. The difficulty of knowing what is meant, he adds, "points to the fact that the term 'history' is an extremely slippery one."

[4]H. Butterfield, *Christianity and History* (London: G. Bell & Sons Ltd., 1949), p. 3.

[5]*ibid.*, p. 119.

[6]Two terms which are often paired are the "Jesus of history" and

yet another way, the problem is that of showing how the knowledge we have by historiography is related to the knowledge we have by faith.

Other ages have had the problem of Jesus posed for them in other forms; but it could well be argued that, however differently stated, the question at the heart of every question has been the one which we are addressing. It might be contended, for instance, that though in the fifth century the problem of Jesus was posed in a way that called for some conception that could comprehend two "natures", what lay at the heart of it was just this conviction that Jesus was both like and unlike other men. Such a contention, and similar ones in respect of other centuries, are certainly possible; and they afford material for studies that would enhance our understanding of Christian thought in the past and disclose an underlying concern in Christians' search for truth. But it is not along that line that our present study will proceed. We shall be concerned with what has already been stated as the core of the problem of Jesus today: the relationship between the historian's Jesus and the believer's Jesus. This will include considering whether any such distinction is justified.

Three considerations in particular point to the importance of these questions.

The first lies in the fact that Christians are bound

---

the "Christ of faith", which appear to have originated with D. F. Strauss (cf. the title of his book, *Der Christus des Glaubens und der Jesus der Geschichte*, published in 1865). Since the term, "Jesus of history", became the symbol of a particular type of assessment of Jesus, it may be noted that Strauss attached to it a significance rather like that given the term "historical Jesus" in these pages. See *infra*, pp. 20-1.

to engage in reflection upon their faith in Jesus Christ as the supreme revelation of God. It is thus that theology arises, and no Christian can escape being a theologian. Elsewhere I have said:

Such reflection, whether we are conscious of it or not, begins at the moment when faith begins. While we usually speak of men who are preparing themselves for the Ministry as "students of theology", we are all of us, in so far as we are Christians, students of theology to some extent, for we cannot help reflecting upon the faith which is ours. The degree to which we carry this reflection and set it out in systematic form is determined by the opportunities and demands of the situation in life which we occupy. It is because these, both opportunities and demands, are greatest in the case of a Minister that the Church demands evidence of a high degree of self-application to this sort of reflection from those who present themselves for Ordination, and not because it is supposed that Ministers have a different sort of experience from other Christians, or are more pious, or are of greater intellectual capacity, than they are.[7]

This being so, reflection by Christians concerning the person in whom their faith has its origin is inevitable; and it is at that point that there arises the problem we are to discuss. For, as we have already noted, this person is susceptible to assessment by historiographical science in the same way as many another figure of the past.

[7]"The Place of Theology in the Church", *The Reformed Theological Review*, vol. XI (1952), p. 52.

No doubt there are some Christians (those for whom opportunities and demands have not pointed the question in this way) who have not had cause to wonder how the historical Jesus is related to the Christ of faith; but these must be few. And the *milieu* in which the thinking of most people today is set—one dominated by a spirit of critical enquiry—is a potent factor in reducing the number.

The fact that people outside the circle of Christian believers often point to this problem is another reason for regarding it as an important one. That religious belief rests on a "historical basis" which cannot be enquired into along the same lines as other "historical" things is an assertion leading to bewilderment, doubt, and even downright ridicule. He who would proclaim the Christian Gospel should see that he does not compromise it by presenting it as something that can be accepted only at the expense of intellectual integrity. There is therefore an apologetic motive for seeking a solution to our problem.

The task of apologetics is in these days seldom, if ever, conceived as that of offering a rational alternative to faith; nor is it considered by serious thinkers that theology should serve as the handmaid of apologetics. Thus to advance the apologetic motive is not to advocate such motives as underlay the *Leben-Jesu-Forschung*, in which what was taken to be the attitude of intelligent people outside the circle of Christian believers was allowed to dictate to those within it concerning what they should, or should not, say about their Lord and Master. Apologetics is, as Brunner says (though he prefers to speak of *Eristik* rather than of *Apologetik*), "the intellectual discussion of the Christian faith with present-day doctrines and ideologies which have set themselves against the Church's message", and has as part of its work the

> proving that the hostile attacks . . . on the Biblical message as being contrary to reason, opposed to culture, scientifically untenable etc. are based upon errors, due either to the confusion of rationalism with reason, of positivism with science, of a critical with a sceptical attitude, or out of ignorance of what the Bible actually teaches.[8]

What matters in apologetics, says Brunner, is not "defence" but "attack"; and it is in such a spirit that Christian thought is called upon to apply itself to the problem of Jesus today. It cannot avoid this problem without compromising its *apologia* for the Gospel, and stultifying its own appreciation of the truth. For what Wilder has written concerning "the symbols and sacraments of the faith" is true also of the historical basis of the faith: namely, that "they mean much in the house of worship, but they will wither and be stifled there unless their original vital relation to all men and to the public secular life of all men is constantly refreshed."[9]

A third reason for considering it important is that the problem looms large in contemporary discussion.

The age which saw the identification of the historical Jesus with the Christ of faith (assuming that the historical person must have been demonstrably identifiable as the Redeemer celebrated in the creeds and liturgies of the Church) was succeeded by one which identified

---

[8]Emil Brunner, *Die Christliche Lehre von Gott* (Zurich: Zwingli-Verlag, 1953) p. 107. *The Christian Doctrine of God.* Trans. Olive Wyon (London: Lutterworth Press, 1949), pp. 98-9.

[9]Amos N. Wilder, *Otherworldliness and the New Testament* (New York: Harper Brothers, 1954), p. 95.

the Christ of faith with the historical Jesus[10] (assuming that any suggestion of the Redeemer being different from such a person as contemporary historiographical science showed Jesus to be was a distortion, and so only a hindrance to faith). This age of liberalism was in turn succeeded by one in which the two are separated—either because it is considered that faith must be immune from the contingent views of the historians, or because it is considered that it is impossible to recover any reliable picture of the historical Jesus. In some instances, both these reasons operate.

This is the climate in which the theologian of today has to work, though there are signs that circles where such an attitude found most general acceptance now include scholars who consider that some things can be known about the historical Jesus, and that faith must take account of them.[11]

Needless to say, no "age" of thought is chronologically water-tight, and there are today representatives of each of the views suggested, as well as of some others. The variety of views, the conflicts between them, and the nature of those receiving greatest attention at the present time underline the fact that contemporary Christian thinking regards our problem as genuinely important.

The approach taken in the following pages begins

[10]At this point the term "Jesus of History" would be in the (English) idiom.

[11]e.g., Günther Bornkamm, Ernst Fuchs and Ernst Käsemann. For an account in English of this development on the Continent, see James M. Robinson, *A New Quest of the Historical Jesus* (London: S.C.M. Press Ltd., 1959). Cf. Ogden's contention that Bultmann has always maintained this. R. Bultmann, *Existence and Faith*, trans. and intr. Schubert M. Ogden (Cleveland: World Publ. Co., 1961), p. 12.

with noting some things which have been said in recent years concerning the picture of Jesus presented in the New Testament (chapter I). There is then considered (along with the nature of historical knowledge generally) what historiographical status any picture of Jesus might have (chapter II), and this is followed by discussion of the place of faith in historical knowledge (chapter III). Notice is then taken of the contribution made by the school of demythologizing (chapter IV); a final chapter (V) states some conclusions suggested by what precedes it.

The thesis maintained is that the picture of Jesus held by the Christian, which is to some extent made what it is by the part which the Christian's peculiar relationship to Jesus plays in establishing it, can lay just claim to being a picture of what Jesus actually was. In other words, the Christian's picture is as accurate a picture as can be had of the historical Jesus.

While a good deal of what follows is concerned precisely with making clear what can be meant by certain words and phrases, it is desirable to note here the ways in which some that occur fairly frequently are used.

The term *event* is used to denote something which has happened in the past, irrespective of anyone's apprehension of it. *Fact* is used to denote what the historian knows of something which has happened in the past.

It is clear that there must be some relationship between an event and a fact; otherwise all hope of historical knowledge would have to be abandoned. It is equally clear that an event and a fact cannot be the same thing, for (to mention the most obvious difference) the event taking place, and the historian knowing about it, do not occur at the same time. Nor, unless it be supposed that a historian can have perfect knowledge of what happened (a patently absurd supposition), is the relationship one of co-extensiveness: a complete description of the event would include features not in the fact (and *vice versa*, if the possibility of error on the part of the historian is admitted to consideration, as well as for other reasons which will appear as our discussion proceeds).

Although so brief a statement may suggest ignorance of the kind of discussion which can surround the term, the relationship between a fact and an event can be characterized as one of essential analogy. By this it is meant that there is a resemblance (and not a fortuitous resemblance) of the fact to the event. That is to say, if the event is characterized as being a, b, c, d etc. to n, any fact related to it must be characterized as being at least some of these. In so far as a fact may be p, q, r, it is (unless it is also a, b, c, etc. to some extent) a fact unrelated to this event. If the historian thinks that it is a fact related to this event, he is mistaken: we should say that his fact is false.

If it be asked in what way any historian can determine the extent to which his fact matches the event, the answer is that he does so in the same way as he judges the truth or falsity of any statement which purports to describe reality: by considering it along with other statements which purport to describe the same reality, and accepting as true which of them he sees to conform to the evidence. By such choices is the fund of one's knowledge built up. And as a man does not need to possess all truth in order to judge whether some particular statement is true, he does not need to know everything about the event in order to judge whether some particular fact is a true one. The historian's knowledge of events is limited to his facts, and he has no way of going beyond facts in order to determine whether any particular fact is true.

The term *historiography* is used to denote the process of arriving at knowledge of what has happened in the past. This use is wider than the origins of the word suggest[12] but it is easy to see how enquiry into the past should be associated in the first place with writing about the past, and the use of the word with this broader connotation is becoming common. Moreover, the use of it in this sense leaves us free to use the word *history* to refer to what has happened (sometimes, more strictly, what we know of what has happened) in the past as distinct from the process of arriving at knowledge of it. *Historiographical science* is used to designate the carrying out of this process by those especially skilled in doing so, or the principles by which they carry it out. *Historian* is used of anyone who is endeavouring to arrive at knowledge of the past.[13]

The term *historical Jesus* denotes all that Jesus was during his life-time. It is not used in the same sense as the term *Jesus of history*, which has become synonymous with a particular assessment of the person of Jesus.[14] To say at this stage just what features of the

---

[12]The Latin *historiographus* (representing the Greek ἱστοριογράθος) appeared in the fourth century A.D. to denote a writer of history. Alexander Souter, *A Glossary of Later Latin to 600 A.D.* (Oxford; The Clarendon Press, 1949), p. 175.

[13]cf. the broad connotation given to the term "theologian", *supra*, p. 14. We might say, in a parallel way, that the "historiographer" is one, the opportunities and demands of whose station in life are greater than those of most other "historians".

[14]See *supra*, note 5 on p. 12, and *infra* Chapter I, pp. 30-1.

New Testament picture can be accepted as having truly belonged to the historical Jesus would be to anticipate a good deal of our later discussion; let it be said baldly here, therefore, that the term historical Jesus denotes all that Jesus is known to have been from his birth to the end of his life on earth.[15]

A recent writer has pointed to an ambiguity in the use of the term, "the historical Jesus". It is not, he says, "simply identical with 'Jesus' or 'Jesus of Nazareth', as if the adjective 'historical' were a meaningless addition", but is used in the technical sense of "things in the past which have been established by objective scholarship." In the nineteenth century it was assumed that objective historical scholarship could (in theory at least) envisage all of reality, and therefore that "the reconstruction of his biography by means of objective historical method" coincided with "Jesus as he actually was".[16] While the tendency among contemporary theologians is to use the term in the former of these two senses, we are using it in the latter.

The term *Christ of faith* denotes the object of the faith of a Christian. It is used particularly whenever there is any suggestion that the presence of faith has occasioned a picture of Jesus different from that which would have been present to the consciousness of the Christian had he (*per impossibile*) not had faith.

---

[15]We are avoiding discussion at this point of the question whether such phenomena as the resurrection and ascension can *ever* be the subject of historiographical science.

[16]James M. Robinson, *op. cit.*, pp. 26-32.

I

The New Testament Picture

NO ONE WILL QUESTION the statement that the figure of Jesus dominates the New Testament. It is true that only four of the twenty-seven books give anything approaching an ordered account of his life; but the material in these four amounts to all but a half of the total, and the other books are just as plainly concerned to give their readers information about Jesus or his significance. Nor will anyone question the further statement that those who wrote in the New Testament supposed that they were writing about a historical figure.

Thus every book of the New Testament provides its own measure of information concerning the picture of the historical Jesus entertained by Christians of that time. It is however to the Gospels that we must look particularly for details of that picture, and when any question is raised concerning the historical soundness of what the New Testament has to say about him, these four books are the subject of chief consideration.

In this chapter we shall review four of the positions which have been taken up during the last hundred years. We shall at the same time be noticing the

significant literature and disclosing factors for which
any who attempt to understand the historical Jesus
must show regard. The chapter will conclude with
a tentative assessment which will set the stage for
subsequent chapters.

The View that Jesus did not Exist

Our consideration of attitudes towards the historical
soundness of the New Testament picture will obey
the dictates of logic, if not those of contemporary
interest, and begin with the view that Jesus did not
exist at all.[1]

During the last century many have put forward
this view, including some scholars of considerable
renown. Today it is practically a lost debate, although
present-day advocates of this view are not unknown.[2]

---

[1]The use of the term "Christ-myth" in this connection is to be
distinguished from its use by a few recent writers (chief among
them Fritz Buri) who, though regarding historical knowledge
about Jesus as irrelevant, do not deny his existence.

[2]The following constitute the most influential presentations of this
view. Bruno Bauer, *Christus und die Cäsaren. Der Ursprung des
Christentums aus dem römischen Griechentum* (Berlin, 1877). Bauer's
earlier position was that the actual existence of Jesus is prob-
lematical, and only of significance as awakening into life the
Messianic idea; the transition may be seen in his *Kritik der
evangelischen Geschichte der Synoptiker* (Leipzig, 1841–2) and *Kritik
der Evangelien und Geschichte ihres Ursprungs* (Berlin, 1850-1851).
Albert Kalthoff, *Das Christusproblem. Grundlinien zu einer Sozial-
theologie* (Leipzig, 1902); *Die Entstehung des Christentums. Neue
Beitrage zum Christusproblem* (Leipzig, 1904); E. T. *The Rise of
Christianity* (London, 1907). As with Bauer, this is a later devel-
opment; cf. *Das Leben Jesu* (Berlin 1880), which presents a view
similar to that of contemporary liberals. Arthur Drews, *The
Christ Myth; Witnesses to the Historicity of Jesus.* J. M. Robertson,
Pagan Christs; Christianity and Mythology. William Benjamin
Smith, *Der Vorchristliche Jesus* (1906), only portions of which have

To deny the existence of Jesus involves discounting a considerable amount of evidence which suggests that he did exist, and it may be sufficient treatment of the view here to remind ourselves of what that evidence is.[3]

There are the Gospels themselves, all four of which were completed well within a hundred years of the death of Jesus, and which scholarly investigation has shown to be the outcome of several earlier documents, or at least of oral traditions from an earlier period. All these assert that Jesus said and did certain things: that is, that at a particular time he was actually in existence.

There are the other books of the New Testament: the Acts, the Epistles and the Revelation, some of which are of earlier date than the Gospels, and all of which (whatever judgment we pass on what they make of him) show a belief that, at a period within the

been included in the E.T., *The Pre-Christian Jesus.* Prosper Alfaric, *Pour comprendre la vie de Jésus* (1929). P.-L. Couchoud, *Jésus, Mythe ou Histoire?* (1924), *Histoire de Jésus* (1944). Some present-day Russian writers (whose scholarly integrity may be doubted) have taken up the cudgels on behalf of this view. The recent editing by Addison Gulick of a MS of W. B. Smith, *The Birth of the Gospel; A Study of the Origin and Purport of the Primitive Allegory of the Jesus* (New York: Philosophical Library Inc., 1957), and the presentation by Gulick of a copy to the Library of the University of Queensland show that some people still have an interest in the propagation of this view.

[3]Notable among treatments of the evidence are: Johannes Weiss, *Jesus: Mythos oder Geschichte* (Tübingen: J. C. B. Mohr, 1910); F. C. Conybeare, *The Historical Christ* (London: Watts & Co., 1914); Joseph Klausner, *Jesus of Nazareth* (London: George Allen & Unwin Ltd., 1925); Maurice Goguel, *La Vie de Jésus* (Paris: Payot, 1932), E. T., *Life of Jesus* (London: George Allen & Unwin Ltd., 1933); Ch. Guignebert, *Jésus* (Paris, 1933); E. T., *Jesus* (1935); Roderic Dunkerley, *Beyond the Gospels* (Harmondsworth: Penguin Books Ltd., 1957).

life-time of at least some of the writers, there had lived a man named Jesus, and show here and there a knowledge of details consonant with those recorded in the Gospels.

There is the existence of a body of early Christian literature other than that contained in the canon, some of which was written before some of the New Testament. Notable here are the works of the Apostolic Fathers, but account must also be taken of the "apocryphal" Gospels and the "heretical" writings which have been known for a long time, as well as of the recently discovered documents from Nag-Hammadi.[4] Of all this literature, so varied in content, style and intention, it may be said generally that it adds little or nothing to our knowledge of Jesus. Nonetheless it must be recognized as evidence of a widespread conviction that such a man existed.

There is non-Christian evidence in the form of passing references made to him in the writings of contemporary historians. Josephus, in his *Jewish Antiquities*, written in the last decade of the first century, has two references to Jesus; both are very brief and seem to have been tampered with by Christians, though it can hardly be denied that the original text disclosed some awareness of the existence of Jesus.[5] Tacitus, writing in about 115 A.D. speaks disparagingly of the "Christiani" and knows that the name was derived from "Christus" who was condemned

---

[4]See Jean Doresse, *The Secret Books of the Egyptian Gnostics*, trans. Philip Mairet (London: Hollis & Carter Ltd., 1959), especially pp. 197-238.

[5]XVIII, iii, 3; xx, ix, 1. See Dunkerley, *op. cit.*, pp. 35–47. Cf. Conybeare, *op. cit.*, p. 156, and Klausner, *op. cit.*, p. 556, on the suspected additions. The references to Jesus in Josephus' *Jewish War* occur only in the Slavonic version.

to death by Pontius Pilate.[6] A reference in Suetonius[7] who lived from 65 to 135, and the early second century correspondence between Pliny the Younger and the Emperor Trajan,[8] are evidence for the existence of the Christian movement, and to that extent bear upon the question whether Jesus himself actually existed.

There are references to Jesus in the Talmud. Günther Bornkamm considers that it "betrays no independent knowledge whatever and is nothing but a polemical and tendentious misrepresentation of the Christian tradition."[9] Ethelbert Stauffer thinks differently, and uses the Talmud quite extensively (along with other non-biblical evidence) in his chronological account of the life of Jesus.[10] The truth lies between these two, and in the attitude of Joseph Klausner who remarks that though the references are "very few" and "of little historical value, since they partake rather of the nature of vituperation and polemic against the founder of a hated party than of objective accounts," they are evidence that this founder of a hated party did actually exist.[11]

Others may advance aditional lines of evidence; Dunkerley, for example, wants to attach some value to what is said about Jesus in Moslem tradition,[12] but the evidence to be advanced along the five lines already

---

[6] *Annales*, xv, 44.
[7] *The Twelve Caesars*, xxv, dealing with Claudius, who reigned from 41 to 54.
[8] *Plinii et Trajani Epistulae*, xcvi, xcvii.
[9] G. Bornkamm, *Jesus of Nazareth*, trans. I. and F. McLuskey with J. M. Robinson (New York: Harper & Row, 1960), p. 28.
[10] E. Stauffer, *Jesus and His Story*, trans. Dorothea M. Barton (London: S.C.M. Press Ltd., 1960), *passim*.
[11] Klausner, *op. cit.*, pp. 18–19. He points out on p. 46 that the first generation of the Tannaim do not seem to have shown the same bitterness as was later displayed.
[12] Dunkerley, *op. cit.*, pp. 145–54.

mentioned is such that even what Conybeare called
"a mere preposterous superfetation of a disordered
imagination"[13] cannot shift.

Before leaving consideration of this view we shall
note—not only because of their interest but also
because of their bearing upon any judgment that we
ourselves may make concerning the New Testament
picture of Jesus—three opinions which are held concerning its origin.

According to Conybeare the blame for the emergence
of such a view must be laid at the door of orthodoxy
which, he says,

by refusing to apply in the field of so-called sacred
history the canons by which in other fields truth
is discerned from falsehood, by beatifying credulous ignorance and anathematizing scholarship
and common sense, has surrounded the figure
of Jesus with such a nimbus of improbability that
it seems not absurd to some critics of today to
deny that he ever lived.[14]

The laity, he says in another place, "are so justly
suspicious of the evasions and *arrière-pensées* of orthodox apologists that they are ready to accept any wild
and unscholarly theory that labels itself Rationalist.[15]

Klausner writes:

When we look afresh into all that has been said of
these three (i.e. the Gospels, Jesus and Christianity) during the first twenty years of this century,
we come to the conclusion that nearly all the
many Christian scholars, and even the best of
them, who have studied the subject deeply, have
tried their hardest to find in the historic Jesus

---

[13]Conybeare, *op. cit.*, pp. 195-6.
[14]Conybeare, *op. cit.*, p. 1, see also pp. 128, 168.   [15]*ibid*, pp.128-9.

something which is not Judaism; but in his actual history they have found nothing of this whatever, since this history is reduced almost to zero. It is therefore no wonder that at the beginning of this century there has been a revival of the eighteenth and nineteenth century view that Jesus never existed.[16]

In Sydney Cave's opinion, the blame must be laid at the door of those (especially in the latter half of the nineteenth century) who were unwilling to accept anything in the Gospels which gave Jesus more than human greatness.

When the fantastic theory was again put out that Jesus never lived, the impression it created for a time in Germany was itself a proof of the precariousness of the over-modernized reconstruction of his life and teaching. For that theory was a reduction to absurdity of the arbitrary methods by which the Gospels had been treated by many scholars.[17]

We may sum up the situation by saying that three factors played their part in the production of this extraordinary view: an inadequate consideration of the data by those who held the view, a conservatism which would allow critical thought no place at all, and a criticism which, suspicious of all conservative presuppositions, remained blind to its own. They must be guarded against continually in every attempt to find the historical Jesus.

[16]Klausner, *op. cit.*, pp. 105–6.
[17]Sydney Cave, *What Shall We Say of Christ?* (London: Hodder & Stoughton Ltd., 1932), p. 23. This opinion had earlier been expressed by Albert Schweitzer, *The Quest of the Historical Jesus* (third English edition, London: A. and C. Black Ltd., 1954), pp. 305, 318.

The View of Liberalism

At the dawn of this century there was published in Germany a series of lectures which were "both a symptom and a source of influence: a symptom of the direction in which liberal Protestantism had been and was still travelling, and the source of an influence which was widely exerted upon liberal theology during the first two decades of the twentieth century."[1]

These were the lectures of Adolf von Harnack on "The Essence of Christianity",[2] and they are regarded by many as the classical exposition of the view we are now to consider.

As far as the picture of Jesus is concerned, the liberal view may be characterized broadly as the "Jesus of history" movement[3]—not that it alone of the estimates of the person of Jesus takes note of the fact that he lived in history, nor that all those classed as belonging to the movement agree in what they say about Jesus; the phrase is used generally to designate those who consider that there is incompatibility between "the Jesus of history" and "the Christ of the creeds", and that it is the former to whom we must go.[4]

The liberal position in regard to the New Testament picture regards Jesus as one who, himself enjoying a

---

[1]G. V. Jones, "Harnack's *Das Wesen des Christentums*", *The Expository Times*, vol. LXVI (1954–55), p. 100.

[2]Adolf von Harnack's *Das Wesen des Christentums*, Leipzig: 1900. An E. T. published a year later had the title *What is Christianity?*

[3]German: *Leben-Jesu-Bewegung* or -*Forschung*, or simply *Historismus*.

[4]Not all who make such a distinction belong to this school. Some note an incompatibility, but claim that it is the latter to whom we must turn.

more than ordinary experience of God through trusting completely in him, taught others to do the same, and gathered about himself a band of disciples. After the hostility of the religious leaders of his people had resulted in his being crucified, his disciples, convinced that the influence of so sublime a life could not be ended there, felt him to be still alive and continued in the fellowship which they had known during his life-time. Before long there grew up within this fellowship beliefs concerning him which were without historical basis. His deeds of service for others became miracles of healing, the experience of his continuing influence became the story that he had left his grave on the third day, and the recognition of the unusually close fellowship with God which he had enjoyed became the conviction that he was in fact a divine being, while the extension of the fellowship to include Gentiles meant that these brought with them ideas of divinity with which they quickly proceeded to overlay the Master of beloved memory. When the time came for some of the fellowship to write accounts of his life and of the early Church, all these tendencies, which by now had so played their part that some of those who wrote had never known a gospel free of them, were reflected in the accounts they gave of the historical events. And the tendencies thus enshrined in the New Testament were carried to further extremes by the Fathers, whose creeds represent degrees of metaphysical speculation undreamed of by Jesus and his first followers.

Among those who have felt that the Jesus of history can and should be separated from the Christ of faith, there have been many different shades of opinion. Some consider that the chief perverter of the simple

Galilean gospel was the apostle Paul, others that later creeds, ostensibly based on his statements, misrepresent him; some hold that the New Testament picture of Jesus, though unhistorical, is to be recognized as an honest, and to some extent successful attempt to express his greatness, others that this picture displays a manner of distortion deplorable and culpable; some insist that the early Church's formulae need filling with new content, others that there can be no advance towards the truth until all the old forms of expression are scrapped completely. But the underlying thesis of liberal thinkers is recognizably the same; their point of view has had and continues to have a wide influence, and many of them have made to the life of the Church at large, as well as to Christian scholarship, contributions of outstanding value.

Those who contended for such a view were able to cite a number of supporting factors.

(a) Christian thinking generally has always been anxious to assert that Jesus was fully human. "Consubstantial with us concerning the manhood," says the Chalcedonian Symbol: a man as we are men. Therefore, it was considered on this view, he was limited as we are limited: to think otherwise is to deny that Jesus was truly a man. This concern for the Saviour's real humanity led on to the conviction that errors must have crept into those passages in the New Testament which suggest that Jesus possessed powers not possessed by us; hence nothing but good would follow the removal of such errors.

(b) It is very often the case that adoration of a hero gives rise to exaggeration of his character and capabilities. Here, it was thought, is a very likely cause of what appear as distortions in the New Testament picture of Jesus. Remembering the power of his personality or aware of the way in which his influence was still to be felt, his followers could think of no title too great, no rank too exalted, for him, and such they proceeded to ascribe to him. Moreover, the first Christians had little interest in the personal life of Jesus; they regarded his return on the clouds as imminent, and were more concerned with waiting in eager hope for their final redemption.

(c) The findings of biblical criticism were held to give added support to this way of thinking; indeed they are still regarded by some as the chief cause of it. It is conceded on all sides that, underlying the Gospels as we have them today, were earlier documents, or at least oral traditions, which the writers used each in his own way. Underlying those documents and traditions there were doubtless others again, and in the process of passing them on embellishment was inevitable. Of particular significance was the fact that the first three Gospels are synoptic in their presentation while it is the fourth Gospel, standing apart from the synoptic tradition and of later date, which records the most extravagant claims made for, or by, Jesus. The same process of biblical criticism made it clear, too, that the New Testament writings are not even avowedly impartial writings, but were penned for a purpose—a purpose which has led to misrepresentation of the historical figure.

(d) The whole outlook of the age which saw the zenith of liberalism tended to favour the production of a Saviour like him whom this movement unfolded. The idea of the innate goodness of men carried with it the idea that all men needed was an example of the highest and best and they would quickly follow it, while the accrediting to him of supernatural powers was an affront to an age characterized by a spirit of scientific enquiry and self-determination.

This, then, is the liberal view, and the grounds upon which it chiefly rested; and there can be no denying its wide influence, the Herculean labours of biblical criticism and theological enquiry which it inspired, and the admirable qualities of Christian character among its supporters. Nor can there be any denying that it gives rise to questions of historiographical procedure which no assessment of the New Testament picture of Jesus can afford to neglect.

Nonetheless, a re-examination of the grounds upon which this position rested has resulted in a general departure from it.

(a) To say that Jesus was a man is not to say that he must fit precisely the mould which what we know of men causes us to construct. The supporters of the liberal view assumed too readily that the men they could see about them are normative for all men. In particular, they thought that Western civilized man was representative, or the best type of manhood; and so, as George Tyrrell said of Harnack, the Christ that they see "looking back through nineteen centuries of Catholic darkness, is only the reflection of a liberal Protestant face seen at the bottom of a deep well."[5]

The knowledge that is to be gained concerning the unusual powers possessed by some men (even some Western civilized men, to say nothing of their greater incidence among Eastern and primitive peoples), in

[5]George Tyrrell, *Christianity at the Cross-roads*, p. 44; cited by D. M. Baillie, *God Was in Christ*, p. 40.

the way of exorcism, telepathy, psycho-kinesis and all that is called generally "extra-sensory perception",[6] might have caused liberal theologians to be rather less confident in their assertions as to what a man, *qua* man, could or could not have done; while the case of Jesus in particular should have led them to wonder whether F. W. Robertson was not right when he remarked "exceptional manifestations of psychic and spiritual force . . . were only to be expected in a being of exceptional elevation and fullest capacity."[7]

(b) It is questionable whether the worship which his first followers gave to Jesus would have led them to the sort of misrepresentation which the liberal theologians attributed to them. More than fifty years ago P. T. Forsyth pointed out:

> We could not speak of Jesus with any respect if his influence not only could not protect his first followers from idolatry in placing him where they did—beside God in their worship—but actually prompted that idolatry. If they included Christ in his own Gospel, then *he* did. It was not in the teeth of him that they made him an object of faith and worship along with the Father. They could never have treated him, those disciples who had been with him, in a way which would have horrified him as much as some apostles were horrified at the attempt to worship them at Lystra. If they found him Saviour through death from sin, found him the Son of God and Eternal

---

[6] See, for instance, the discussion in J. B. Rhine, *The Reach of the Mind* (Harmondsworth; Penguin Books Ltd., 1948) and Lewis Spence, *Second Sight; Its History and Origins* (London: Rider & Company, 1951).

[7] This statement occurs in one of Robertson's sermons, the precise reference of which I have mislaid.

Christ, then he offered himself as such in some form or other.[8]

Nor can we accept unquestioningly the allegation that the New Testament writers had no real interest in the life which Jesus lived. One writer's statement of the trouble to which he went in the preparation of his Gospel,[9] another's assertion that there had been no following of cunningly devised fables,[10] and the declaration by a third concerning the first-hand nature of his testimony[11] point to the currency of statements at variance with those in the New Testament, and indicate that at least some of the New Testament writers were anxious to show themselves reliable witnesses. We may not regard them as such in every particular, but we are bound to notice that their motives included a desire to have certain things about Jesus put accurately. We are bound to notice also that a similar desire underlay the later refusal to admit certain "Gospels" to the canon.

(c) While criticism of the New Testament has done much to disclose the nature of its writings and in particular to show how the Gospels are related to each other and to earlier documents (or traditions), it is not generally conceded now, as was once declared so confidently, that a chronological progression in dogma is discernible. Instead, it is considered that the Christ of the creeds is implicit in even the earliest of the New Testament writings, and that "the riddle of the New Testament" lies in the figure of Jesus himself. As

[8]P. T. Forsyth, *The Person and Place of Jesus Christ* (London: Hodder & Stoughton Ltd., 1909), p. 207.

[9]Luke 1. 1–4. See also the short article by John Baker, "Luke the Critical Evangelist", *The Expository Times*, vol. LXVIII (1956–7), pp. 123-5.

[10]II Peter 1.16.   [11]John 19.35; I John 1.1–3.

Hoskyns and Davey say in their book with that title: Any historical reconstruction which leaves an unbridgeable gap between the faith of the primitive Church and the historical Jesus must be both inadequate and uncritical: inadequate, because it leaves the origin of the Church unexplained, and uncritical because a critical sifting of the evidence of the New Testament points towards the life and death of Jesus as the ground of primitive Christian faith, and points in no other direction.[12]

"There was," G. S. Duncan remarks, "a naive readiness among many critics to believe that only the earliest sources could be trusted as history."[13]

The possible consequences of such a line of argument were stated forcefully by Schweitzer, whose remarks concerning Schmiedel and von Soden can be applied to liberal thinkers generally:

They assert that there is no distinction of principle between the way in which the Johannine and the synoptic discourses are composed: the recognition of this was Bruno Bauer's starting point. They propose to find experiences of the Christian community and Pauline teaching reflected in the Gospel of Mark: Bruno Bauer asserted the same. The only difference is that he was consistent, and extended his criticism to those portions of the Gospel which do not present the stumbling-block of the supernatural. Why should these not also contain the theology and the experiences

[12]E. Hoskyns and N. Davey, *The Riddle of the New Testament* (second edition; London: Faber & Faber Ltd., 1936), p. 170.
[13]G. S. Duncan, *Jesus, Son of Man* (London: Nisbet & Co. Ltd., 1948), p. 15.

of the community transformed into history?[14]

It is moreover doubtful whether source criticism did have much influence upon the picture of Jesus which the liberal theologians succeeded in drawing; many of the decisions concerning the authenticity of the narrative are made according to a preconceived picture of what Jesus ought to be rather than in strict accordance with any principles of historiography. It is this basing of the life of Jesus on an ideal picture which is not derived from the Gospels, but stands complete in advance, which has led Cullmann to speak of the liberal position as a continuing form of Docetism.[15]

(d) There is a marked difference between the general outlook of the heyday of liberalism and that of our own day. The bright optimism which believed that progress was inevitable has been replaced by a cynicism which, however to be deplored in some of its manifestations, is realistic in its recognition that men need more than an example to lead them to do good.

For such reasons as these liberalism has in the last score or so of years suffered a serious decline. But it has still some outspoken representatives, and the influence of its postulates, and of the methods of fearless investigation which it encouraged, continues, and not least among those who have contributed most to its downfall.

---

[14]Albert Schweitzer, *op. cit.*, p. 305. Cf. his statement concerning Kalthoff: "The Christ of Kalthoff is nothing else than the Jesus of those whom he combats in such lofty fashion: the only difference is that he draws his figure of Christ in red ink on blotting paper, and because it is red in colour and smudgy in outline, wants to make out that it is something new" (*ibid.*, p. 318).

[51]Oscar Cullmann, *Christ and Time* (London: S.C.M. Press Ltd., 1951), p. 129.

The View of Consistent Eschatology

The liberal position suffered a severe shock at the hands of Albert Schweitzer, who, Bornkamm says, "has erected its memorial, but at the same time delivered its funeral oration."[1]

Whether it is right to conclude, as some have done, that Schweitzer is alone responsible, or more responsible than others for loosening the stranglehold which liberalism had upon Christian scholarship is beyond our present interest. We shall concern ourselves with the view put forward by Schweitzer himself, and the way in which his presentation made possible a new approach to the question of the historical Jesus.

Schweitzer's view can be found in his *Sketch* of the life of Jesus, published in 1901.[2] But it finds more forceful expression in a book which appeared ten years later (and which he intended at first to be only a supplement to the earlier one[3]). This was *The Quest of the Historical Jesus*.[4]

[1]Günther Bornkamm, *op. cit.*, p. 13. Schweitzer, no less than those he criticized, used the gospels as sources for a chronological biography.

[2]*Das Messianitäts- und Leidensgeheimnis. Eine Skizze des Lebens Jesu* (Tübingen: J. C. B. Mohr, 1901). The E. T., *The Mystery of the Kingdom of God, The Secret of Jesus' Messiahship and Passion*, was not published until 1925 (London: A. & C. Black).

[3]A. Schweitzer, *Out of My Life and Thought*, trans. C. T. Campion (New York: The New American Library of World Literature, Inc., 1953), p. 30.

[4]*Von Reimarus zu Wrede* (Tübingen: J. C. B. Mohr, 1906). The E. T., *The Quest of the Historical Jesus; A Critical Study of its Progress from Reimarus to Wrede*, was published in 1910 (London: A. & C. Black). A second, and revised German edition was published in 1913 under the title, *Geschichte der Leben-Jesu-Forschung*, but this has not been translated. The Third English Edition of 1954 differs from the edition of 1910 by the inclusion of an Introduction.

Few writers, over the years since the publication of Schweitzer's *Quest*, have failed to be influenced by him and, though not many of his followers have accepted his contentions in their entirety, Schweitzer himself has not offered any substantial modification of his position. "The decision in favour of eschatology is hardly likely to be questioned again," he has written more recently, although, because of "the difficulties it raises for the traditional Christian faith," the eschatological solution has not succeeded in dominating the latest writing on the life of Jesus, and is not within sight of doing so.[5]

The first eighteen of the twenty chapters of Schweitzer's best-known book are taken up with a survey of eighteenth and nineteenth century attempts to portray the historical Jesus.[6] He considers that these attempts had made it clear, at the end of the nineteenth century, that (accepting the Marcan hypothesis of synoptic origins) the only possible alternatives are a thorough-going scepticism or a thorough-going eschatology:[7] either we must regard the picture of Jesus based on the Marcan narrative as the creation of the evangelist or we must accept it, complete with the eschatological utterances, as an authentic picture of Jesus.

Of the alternatives, Schweitzer accepts the second and regards Jesus as a visionary, the product of Jewish

---

[5]Introduction to *The Quest of the Historical Jesus*, Third English edition, p. xiv.

[6]Hence the title of the book. H. S. Reimarus wrote in 1778 and W. Wrede in 1901. Schweitzer concerns himself almost exclusively with attempts which appeared in German.

[7]German, *konsequente Eschatologie*. It is this which (in order to avoid confusion with other views taking account of the eschatological emphasis in the New Testament) has caused this position to be called that of "thoroughgoing" or "consistent" eschatology.

apocalypticism, convinced that he was the Messiah, and proclaiming from the outset the immediate advent of the kingdom of God. In this expectation he sent out the Twelve and, when their return showed that his expectation was disappointed, he concluded that his own death was necessary for the ushering in of the kingdom. Believing this, Jesus set out for Jerusalem intending to suffer death at the hands of the authorities, and (for so he now considered it to be the will of God) to have concentrated upon himself the sufferings which he had always considered to form part of the mystery of the kingdom of God. He died, believing that he was fulfilling the purposes of God, giving his life for the "many" predestined to share in the king-dom.

At no stage, Schweitzer considers, did Jesus volun-tarily disclose the secret of his Messiahship: it was wrung from him by the pressure of events. At the Transfiguration the three disciples did not learn it from his lips, but in a state of ecstasy in which he shared; and Peter's declaration of his Messiahship in the presence of the other disciples at Caesarea Philippi (which in Schweitzer's view took place *after* the Transfiguration) was a betrayal of the confidence given him on the earlier occasion. The triumphal entry into Jerusalem was not an occasion when Jesus was recog-nized generally as the Messiah; he entered as the prophet Elijah (for to assume a general recognition of the Messiahship at this point makes unintelligible the subsequent happenings of Passion Week). It was precisely the communication of his Messiahship which constituted Judas' betrayal; and it was the priests' going among the crowd telling of this which changed the crowd so quickly from their view of him as a prophet worthy of honour to that of him as a blasphemer deserving of death.

This, according to Schweitzer, is the historical Jesus, "to our time a stranger and an enigma", but one who "means something to our world because a mighty spiritual force streams forth from him and flows through our time also."[8]

There is no doubt that Schweitzer's protest against the attitude that was common among scholars, and against the ideology which underlay it, was as timely as it was telling. But neither its timeliness nor the fascinating manner of his presentation of it should blind us to the defects in Schweitzer's position.

Much in the Gospels shows that Jesus was far from being concerned exclusively with the coming kingdom and that, on the contrary, he saw life in this present world as a good gift of God, to be enjoyed by his children with thankfulness. He who urged men to consider the lilies of the field, who drew the material for his teaching from such things as a father's readiness to give his son what he asks for, to whom the common people, including their children, gladly flocked to hear him, and who by comparison with the Pharisees and with John the Baptist was regarded as rather too ready to enjoy life with all, cannot have been entirely the sort of man Schweitzer has in mind.

Nor is Jesus altogether "to our time a stranger and an enigma". Efforts to make him "by a popular historical treatment" into a figure "sympathetic and universally intelligible to the multitude"[9] must face the criticisms which Schweitzer advances; but the fact remains that there is much which makes a strong appeal to every age, and shows his teaching to be not,

[8] *The Quest of the Historical Jesus*, p. 397.   [9] *op. cit.*, p. 397.

as Schweitzer contended, only an *Interimsethik* but
a teaching relevant to the life we know now. Herbert
G. Wood points out: "When Jesus exhorts his
disciples to love their enemies, he does not base his
appeal on the nearness of the kingdom, but on what
has been called the grand courtesy of God in making
the sun to shine and the rain to fall on the thankful
and the thankless."[10] As A. M. Hunter says bluntly,
Schweitzer makes nonsense of the ethic of Jesus,[11]
for in his view, since the world did not come to an
end as Jesus expected, his ethic can have little relevance
for the twentieth century. In point of fact his ethic
has won universal commendation and, as Hunter
says in another place, Schweitzer's own career is a
glorious refutation of what seems to be the logic of his
theory.[12]

In the third place, Schweitzer's presentation is
unsatisfactory because of the limitations of his exegesis,
which practically begins and ends with Matthew, and
in Matthew with the sayings in 10.23 and 11.12.[13]
Thus he concentrates attention upon those aspects
of Jesus' life and teaching which appear to have been
a source of puzzlement to the very people who were
sufficiently drawn to him to seek to preserve a record
of what he said and did.

There is on Schweitzer's part an assumption that
Jesus accepted without question or amendment the

[10]"Albert Schweitzer and Eschatology", *The Expository Times*, vol.
LXV (1953-4), p. 207.
[11]"The Life of Christ in the Twentieth Century", *The Expository
Times*, vol. LXI (1949-50), p. 132. See also *Interpreting the New
Testament, 1900-50* (London: S.C.M. Press Ltd., 1951), p. 52.
[12]"The Meaning of the Sermon on the Mount", *The Expository Times*,
vol. LXIII (1951-2), p. 177.
[13]A. M. Hunter, *Interpreting the New Testament*, p. 52.

ideas of an apocalyptic Messiah which prevailed in Judaism. The essential weakness of Schweitzer's method, says Richard R. Niebuhr, is that

> he rests his whole explanation upon a reference to the spirit or mentality of the age. He allows no originality or creativity to individuals and groups within a given generation . . . The New Testament can equally well—if not much more easily—be made to show that the primitive community during the first decades of its life was continually re-interpreting its eschatological hopes not only in the light of present circumstances but through the recollected figure of Jesus Christ.[14]

"It was," Niebuhr says again, "not the *Zeitgeist* that declared him Lord of the times any more than it proclaims him as such today."[15]

Nowhere is the limited nature of Schweitzer's exegesis more apparent than in his neglect of the place given in the New Testament to the Resurrection.

> They (Schweitzer and his disciple Werner) regard as the mid-point of the process the future coming of the Messianic age, whereas the mid-point of time in the entire New Testament and *already for Jesus* is rather the historical work of Jesus himself . . . It is simply not true that Primitive Christianity has the same eschatological orientation as does Judaism . . . The primary thing is not the eschatological expectation, but this conviction concerning the resurrection . . . Since the juxtaposition of "already fulfilled" and "not yet

---

[14]Richard R. Niebuhr, *Resurrection and Historical Reason; A Study of Theological Method* (New York: Charles Scribner's Sons, 1957), p. 133.

[15]*ibid*, p. 134.

fulfilled" is already present with Jesus, it is clearly impossible to represent the Primitive Christian solution, in contrast to the eschatological attitude of Jesus himself, as a "solution inspired by embarrassment".[16]

A further defect of this view is its assumption that Jesus' recognition of his own death as the decisive point in the divine plan of salvation excludes the possibility of a time interval between this death and the Parousia. Morgenthaler has remarked that the saying in Matthew 10 (upon which Schweitzer leans so heavily) is to be read "as an expectation for the near future, but not for the very near future",[17] while Cullmann points out that there are a number of sayings[18] which show that such an interval (whether he expected it to be a short one or a long one is not essential) is precisely what Jesus anticipated.[19]

That Jesus did not believe history would come to an end shortly after his death is maintained also by C. H. Dodd[20] who takes Schweitzer and his followers to task for

> proposing a compromise. In the face of one set
> of sayings which appeared to contemplate the
> coming of the kingdom of God as future, and
> another set which appeared to contemplate it
> as already present, [Schweitzer] offered an

[16]O. Cullmann, *Christ and Time*, pp. 85–6.
[17]Morgenthaler, *Kommendes Reich* cited by Herbert G. Wood, *The Expository Times*, vol. LXV (1953–4), p. 208.
[18]e.g., Mark 14.62; 13.10; 2.18; 14.28.
[19]Cullman, *Christ and Time*, pp. 149–50. Cullman mentions the sayings indicated, and refers to W. G. Kummel, *Verheissung und Erfüllung*, 1945, and W. Michaelis, *Der Herr verzieht nicht seine Verheissung*, 1942.
[20]C. H. Dodd, *The Parables of the Kingdom* (revised edition; London: Collins (Fontana Books) 1961), pp. 82, 115.

interpretation which represented it as coming very, very soon. But this is no solution.[21]
Brunner points out:

> The imminent expectation of the Parousia in the whole of the New Testament pales into insignificance before the belief that in Jesus Christ the New Age had already dawned—as indeed the message of Jesus himself is permeated through and through with this conviction—and it is clear in the New Testament itself that the "delay" of the Parousia just did not have the effect expected of it according to the "Consistent Eschatology" theories.[22]

While such defects as these preclude acceptance of the view of consistent eschatology, it is possible to appreciate a number of things which our consideration of that view has brought to light. We shall do well to note these before we proceed further in our consideration of the New Testament picture of Jesus.

Schweitzer's presentation has served to remind us that our best understanding of the teaching of Jesus and the events of his life will come as we place them against the background of first century Palestine. F. C. Burkitt reminded readers in the first English edition of the *Quest*: "The true view of the Gospel will be that which explains the course of events in the first century and the second century, rather than that which seems to have spiritual and imaginative value for the twentieth century."[23] And Schweitzer himself said:[24]

[21]*ibid.*, p. 40; cf. p. 131.

[22]F. Brunner, *Die christliche Lehre von Schöpfung und Erlösung* (Zurich: Zwingli-Verlag, 1950), p. 310. E. T., p. 262.

[23]*op. cit.*, preface, p. vii.   [24]*op. cit.*, p. 250.

"Eschatology makes it impossible to attribute modern ideas to Jesus and then by way of 'New Testament Theology' take them back from him as a loan."

We can be grateful too for Schweitzer's demonstration that the tradition of the life of Jesus enshrined in the Gospels is not something easily divided into sections, any of which can then be discarded at will. His argument shows, for example, that the predictions of the Passion and Resurrection are as much a part of primitive tradition as anything else, and that the practice of arbitrarily dismissing features inconvenient to one's hypothesis has as its logical outcome a complete scepticism concerning knowledge of the historical Jesus.

Again, Schweitzer made it plain that any adequate representation of the historical Jesus has to take account of the "other-worldly" factor in his thought and teaching. Schweitzer may have over-estimated its place but he has made plain the fact that it is there, and that the significance of Jesus is not exhausted when one has succeeded in drawing up his system of ethics.

What is to be noted in this connection is that there is no necessary conflict (although Schweitzer's presentation suggests that there is) between the "this-worldly" and the "other-worldly" aspects of the thought and teaching of Jesus. As G. S. Duncan has pointed out:

> So long as history is regarded as essentially a succession of events which follow one after the other in a time sequence, the Last Things will be the things which come at the end of the sequence; they will be last in the sense that they are not followed by other events. But if we conceive history as the Jews conceived it, as revealing

in human affairs the working out of a divine purpose, then Last Things may begin long before the end of the time process; they take place at any time when God effectively breaks through into history . . . and if it be the case that the concern of Jesus was to lead men to know that the salvation that God had promised under his covenant with his people was now *a present reality*, if he was announcing, not so much a consummation towards which men should look forward, as a consummation which need not tarry but may be experienced *now*, then his message was eschatological through and through. And the eschatology is to be traced, not merely in sayings like those regarding the coming of the Son of Man on the clouds of Heaven, but in such a word as "Son, thy sins are forgiven."[25]

A term which has been made popular in this connection, and which has helped towards clarification of the matter, is that of C. H. Dodd, who speaks of "realized eschatology" (as opposed to "futurist eschatology"):[26] although history still goes on, and the end is yet to be, the meaning of history has been revealed in the decisive event which has already taken place.[27]

Finally, there is in Schweitzer's presentation a severe criticism of the common notion that dogmatism of any kind must spell the end of historicity. He says:

In order to make the historical possibility of the

[25] *Jesus, Son of Man*, p. 50.
[26] A. M. Hunter suggests "inaugurated" as a better term than "realized". "The Interpretation of the Parables", *The Expository Times*, vol. LXIX (1957–8), p. 102.
[27] C. H. Dodd, *The Apostolic Preaching and its Developments* (new edition reset; London: Hodder & Stoughton Ltd., 1944), appendix, "Eschatology and History", pp. 79–96.

resolve to suffer and the prediction of the sufferings in some measure intelligible, modern theology
has to ignore the prediction of the Resurrection,
which is bound up with them, for this is "dogmatic". This is however not permissible. We
must, as Wrede insists, take the words as they are,
and must not even indulge in ingenious explanations of the "three days". Therefore, the resolve
to suffer and to die are dogmatic; therefore,
according to him, they are unhistorical, and only
to be explained by a literary hypothesis. But the
thoroughgoing eschatological school says they
are dogmatic, and therefore historical, because
they find their explanation in eschatological
conceptions.[28]

We need not at this stage accept or discuss the
"dogmatic, therefore historical" contention;[29] it is
enough to be reminded that a statement is not
necessarily false because it is in accord with
some idea which the writer is known, or believed, to
hold.

All these factors—both those which weigh against
Schweitzer's position and those which show the lasting
values in it—have done much to open up for us a
situation in which the question of the historical Jesus
can be approached in a less biased way.

The View of Form-Criticism

Some forty years ago there appeared the first signs
of another approach to the New Testament picture

---

[28] *The Quest of the Historical Jesus*, p. 385.
[29] Something will be said later concerning the place of the historian's
presuppositions. See *infra*, pp. 115-18.
F.H.J.

of Jesus—one which came to dominate scholarship (particularly Continental scholarship) to almost the same extent as liberalism had done before it, and which A. M. Hunter in 1950 named as the chief reason why scholars of the past twenty-five years had continued so reluctant to produce any "Life" of Jesus comparable with those of previous generations.[1] This was the *Formgeschichtliche Schule*,[2] referred to in English generally (perhaps not quite accurately) as the school of "Form-criticism".[3]

Some words of R. H. Lightfoot will be sufficient

[1] "The Life of Christ in the Twentieth Century", *The Expository Times*, vol. LXI (1949–50), p. 135. See also *Interpreting the New Testament, 1900–1950*, p. 58.

[2] The movement rose under the leadership of such scholars as K. L. Schmidt (*Der Rahmen der Geschichte Jesu*, 1919), Martin Dibelius (*Die Formgeschichte des Evangeliums*, 1919; second edition, 1933; E. T., *From Tradition to Gospel*, 1934; *Gospel Tradition and Christology*, 1935) and Rudolf Bultmann (*Jesus*, 1925; E. T., *Jesus and the Word*, 1934; *Die Geschichte der synoptischen Tradition*, 1921; 2nd edition 1931, 3rd edition 1958, E.T. 1960) who is still regarded by some as the leading writer in this field, though others would put his later writings (e.g. *Offenbarung und Heilsgeschehen*, 1941; *Theologie des Neuen Testaments*, 1949; E.T., 1952 and 1955) in a different category.

[3] Like some other movements in theology, Form-criticism had a considerable influence on the Continent before it was really known in English-speaking countries. Ignorance of the background of Form-criticism, according to C. Leslie Mitton, was the reason why Maurice Goguel's *La Vie de Jésus* seemed "niggardly and disappointing" when the E.T. appeared in 1933: in his diligent and tenacious seeking for the bedrock of history in the Gospel record, says Mitton, Goguel "was attempting a task which most British readers had not realized to be necessary" (Goguel's 'Life of Jesus', *The Expository Times*, vol. LXV (1954–5), p. 259). The leading exponent of Form-criticism in English was R. H. Lightfoot (*History and Interpretation in the Gospels*, 1935); others who made it known include notably: B. S. Easton (*The Gospel Before the Gospels*, 1928; *Christ in the Gospels*, 1930), F. C. Grant (*The Growth of the Gospels*, 1933), Vincent Taylor (*The Formation of the Gospel Tradition*, 1933) and William Manson (*Jesus the Messiah*, 1943).

reminder here of its main tenets. In his Bampton Lectures (1934) he said of the Form critics:

They remind us that the early Church is by no means likely to have expressed itself at once in a literary way, and they believe, first, that in the earliest years memories and traditions of the words and deeds of Jesus were only handed from mouth to mouth, and, secondly, that they were valued, not so much . . . in and for themselves, as for their importance in solving problems connected with the life and needs of the young churches. These needs, they think, would be chiefly concerned with mission preaching, catechetical teaching, demonstration of the content and meaning of the Christian life, refutation of Jewish and other objections, and, perhaps above all, worship. They believe, further, that these memories and traditions . . . would gradually assume a more or less fixed shape, through constant repetition in the churches . . . And, finally they suggest that many of these pre-literary traditions are still discernible in our written Gospels . . . and that to some extent they can be classified according to their type or form.[4]

Form-criticism endeavours to classify the material according to its form, to recover the original form of the material and trace its subsequent changes, and to seek for the life-situation (*Sitz im Leben*) out of which the material arose.[5] The net result, in the hands of many Form critics, is to regard the New Testament

[4]R. H. Lightfoot, *History and Interpretation in the Gospels* (London: Hodder & Stoughton Ltd., 1935), pp. 30–1.

[5]On this three-fold task of Form-criticism, see Vincent Taylor, *The Formation of the Gospel Tradition* (London: Macmillan & Co. Ltd., 1935), pp. 22–8.

picture as affording us very little knowledge of the historical Jesus: the Gospels, in Lightfoot's well-known words, "yield us little more than a whisper of his voice; we trace in them but the outskirts of his ways."[6]

But this sort of sceptical conclusion concerning the New Testament picture requires modification.

E. A. Judge has pointed out how our lack of information and inability to prescribe a satisfactory method of analysis make it very difficult to know just what sort of community the early Christians constituted.[7] There is however sufficient evidence to show

> that at each stage of the movement the initiative lay with persons whose work was in important respects of a scholarly kind, and that they accepted the status in the community that this required, and employed the conventional methods of instructing and organizing their followers.[8]

The exploratory work done by Judge recently thus gives confirmation to the point made by William Manson when he wrote twenty years ago:

> It is an exceedingly dubious analogy which is chosen when the rise and development of the early Christian tradition is explained in terms of processes which have worked in the folk-literature

[6]*op. cit.*, p. 225. "This paragraph attained great notoriety; it proved to have been very unfortunately phrased, coming, as it did, with all the emphasis of a peroration. Lightfoot expected that the allusion to Job 26.14 (R.V.) would be more widely recognized than it was and so his words were frequently understood in a sense rather more extreme than that intended (see Lightfoot's statement in *The Gospel Message of St. Mark*, p. 103). In any case he subsequently modified his views on this subject." D. E. Nineham (ed.) *Studies in the Gospels; Essays in Memory of R. H. Lightfoot* (Oxford: Basil Blackwell, 1955), p. x.
[7]"The Early Christians as a Scholastic Community", *The Journal of Religious History*, vol. 1 (1960–1), pp. 5–6.
[8]*ibid.*, p. 136.

THE NEW TESTAMENT PICTURE

of primitive peoples or in early Hebrew saga. The period which divides Jesus from the composition of Mark is little more than a generation. In two generations from Jesus the literary fixation of the tradition in our Gospels was complete. In the first generation there were persons in the Christian community who had seen and heard the Lord. What is of even greater importance at this point is that the level of intelligence in the original Christian groups and circles must have been relatively high. It rested upon Jewish standards of education, and the conservative mentality of the Beth-ha-Midrash may be considered to offer a closer analogy to that of the Church than the naive creativeness of a primitive story-telling society.[9]

This last point has received particular, and probably exaggerated, attention in recent years from a group of Swedish scholars who consider that the Form critics, in their search for the *Sitz im Leben*, have overlooked the chief feature in it: the care which the first Christians took to memorize, and then pass on in a pure form, the authentic account.[10] "Jesus is the object and subject of a tradition of authoritative and holy words which he himself created and entrusted to his disciples for its later transmission in the epoch between his death and the parousia."[11]

[9]William Manson, *Jesus the Messiah; The Synoptic Tradition of the Revelation of God in Christ: with Special Reference to Form-Criticism* (London: Hodder & Stoughton Ltd., 1943), p. 27.

[10]See, for instance: Harald Riesenfeld, *The Gospel Tradition and its Beginnings: A Study in the Limits of 'Formgeschichte'* (London: A. R. Mowbray & Co. Ltd., 1957); Birger Gerhardsson, *Memory and Manuscript* (Uppsala: Gleerup and Munksgaard, 1961).

[11]Riesenfeld, *ibid*, p. 30.

A good deal of the work of Form-criticism depends upon the assumptions that all the Gospel material can be classified into one or another of the recognized "forms", that from the form in which an incident or saying is recorded can be deduced information concerning its authenticity, and that the *Sitz im Leben* must be a situation which arose in the life of the early Church.[12]

The need for questioning these assumptions is another reason for modifying the picture which the Form critics present. No particular classification of the Gospel material finds general acceptance. It is not the case that we make our judgments concerning the authenticity of elements in the Gospel accounts on the basis of the form in which they are presented to us: where we feel that we can make such judgments, we are much more influenced by their *content*. And there appears a strange perversity on the part of Form critics so that, as D. M. Baillie says,

> it seems seldom to occur to them that the story may have been handed on simply or primarily *because it was true*, because the incident had actually taken place in the ministry of Jesus, and was therefore of great interest to his followers, even if they sometimes failed to understand it.[13]

John McIntyre goes to the root of the matter when he points out that:

---

[12]There may be mentioned also the assumption (held also by Liberalism, and some other movements) that a "historical" interest is incompatible with a homiletic or apologetic one. Such an antithesis is an exaggerated one: a purpose of persuading does not necessarily lead to misrepresentation. Something will be said of the part played in historiography by the historian's purpose, *infra*. pp. 109-11.

[13]D. M. Baillie, *God Was in Christ*, p. 57.

in effect, the controversy between the Form critics and some, at least, of their opponents, does not concern only textual or critical matters; it opens up the much vaster question of the nature, content and locus of revelation.[14]

On the preceding page he says:

Beyond question, fulfilment was an *Ur*-word of the primitive Church, if not in fact the *Ur*-word, for the description of how to understand the 'mission and message' of Jesus Christ. But it was an *Ur*-word in the primitive Church because that was how Jesus first regarded himself. It is, of course, arguable that Jesus was the fulfilment of the Old Testament and that he was not aware of being so. But the problem at once presents itself of defining the sense in which he is the Revelation of God. For if it is the primitive Church which is the first to apprehend Jesus Christ as fulfilment, and if such a conception is projected back into the mind of Jesus Christ by the New Testament writers, then the conclusion follows that Revelation is something that happens in the primitive Church and in the writers of the New Testament, but not in Jesus Christ.[15]

It is no departure from the earlier statement that McIntyre goes to the root of the matter when I go on to say that I believe him to have confused "revelation" and "apprehension of revelation".[16] Granted that the primitive Church was the first to apprehend

[14]John McIntyre, *The Christian Doctrine of History* (Edinburgh: Oliver & Boyd, 1957), p. 48.
[15]*ibid.*, p. 47.
[16]To deny the possibility of distinguishing these two is to make impossible any discussion of a revelation which has taken place in the past.

Jesus Christ as fulfilment, it could still be true that revelation is something that happened in him. It could be that what they were the first to apprehend is what had been the truth all along; he may have been the fulfilment of the Old Testament without being aware of it.

There is disclosed at this point a difference among those classed as Form critics: some consider that, though we cannot attain to much, if any, knowledge of the historical Jesus, it would be a good thing if we could. Others consider that such knowledge would be of no advantage to us anyway.[17] Here lies the root of the matter—"the question of the nature, content and locus of revelation."

The Element of Uniqueness

This consideration of four significant views concerning the New Testament picture of Jesus has made clearer what is involved in making an assessment of it. It is clear that such factors as the predilections of the writers, the nature of the evidence to which they had access and the uses for which they intended their writings must be weighed carefully if the assessment is to be a sound one. Having these matters in mind, we are in a position to make an assessment of our own.

Before doing this, however, we shall pay separate attention to something which looms large in any consideration of the New Testament picture—the uniqueness of Jesus himself. Many passages from

[17]It may be said, generally, that the former attitude is that of the British Form critics, and the latter that of the German, and that in this latter attitude is to be discerned the line that runs from *Formgeschichte* to *Entmythologisierung*.

the Acts and the Epistles could be adduced to support
this; we shall restrict our consideration to the Gospels.
Even those who reduce the historicity of the picture
there to a minimum, and regard as authentic few if
any of the deeds and words attributed to Jesus must
take into consideration at least two factors which are
integral to the picture.

In the first place, there is in this picture the extraordinary influence of Jesus upon other people. "Every
one of the scenes described in the Gospels reveals
Jesus' astounding sovereignty in dealing with situations
according to the kind of people he encounters," says
Günther Bornkamm who goes on to say that, whatever
be the extent to which the various stories have legendary accretions, "the important thing is that in all of
them the same feature recurs, by which the historical
Jesus can be recognized."[1]

A frank estimate of this influence, in G. S. Duncan's
view, is of itself "enough to bring into suspicion, if not
indeed into discredit, some of the essentially humanistic
interpretations of his person which are accepted all
too readily as historical."[2] "If the claims of Jesus
to personal obedience are felt to be amazing," remarks
H. R. Mackintosh, "not less wonderful is the free and
joyous acquiescence with which men respond to his
call."[3]

John Macquarrie suggests that what Jesus aroused
in men was "anxiety" or "dread" (with the peculiar
connotation of these words given them by existen-
tialists). "When Jesus claimed to be the light of the

[1] op. cit., pp. 58, 59.
[2] G. S. Duncan, *Jesus, Son of Man; Studies Contributory to a Modern
Portrait* (London: Nisbet & Co. Ltd., 1948), p. 12.
[3] H. R. Mackintosh, *The Doctrine of the Person of Jesus Christ* (second
edition; Edinburgh: T. & T. Clark, 1913), p. 31.

world, the good shepherd, the true vine (John 8.12; 10.11; 15.1), it is assumed in each case that man is looking for light for his way, a shepherd of souls, a ground of being."[4] Referring to Bultmann's discussion of the Jews' efforts to set aside the uneasiness (*Störung*) which they felt by appealing to their law, their history, and their honour (the familiar world in which they felt at home), Macquarrie says:

> Here he is surely right in pointing out that it must have been a characteristic of the historic Jesus to disturb men . . . The Jews sought to explain away this feature in the person of Jesus, so as to quieten the feeling he had aroused and restore their sense of security in their way of life. No doubt with a different motive, much modern criticism has been equally active in explaining away the numinous elements in the personality of the historic Jesus.[5]

There is, as a second feature of the picture of Jesus which the Gospels present, the fact that he made claims—claims, Mackintosh says, "not so much argued as presupposed"[6]—suggesting that he considered himself to be possessed of more than ordinary significance.[7]

His declaration that "something greater"[8] was present in himself, his belief that many prophets and righteous men had desired to see and hear what his

[4]John Macquarrie, *An Existentialist Theology: A Comparison of Heidegger and Bultmann* (London: S.C.M. Press Ltd., 1955), p. 80.
[5]*ibid.*, pp. 80–1.   [6]Mackintosh, *op. cit.*, p. 32.
[7]See, for a discussion of this whole question based on the Synoptic Gospels, the article by A. W. Argyle, "The Evidence for the Belief that our Lord Himself Claimed to be Divine," *The Expository Times*, vol. LXI (1949–50), pp. 228–32.
[8]Matthew 12.41, 42 = Luke 11.31, 32.

contemporaries saw and heard,[9] his drawing, as
Duncan puts it, of "a life-or-death distinction"[10]
between those who heard his sayings and did them and
those who did them not,[11] between those who confessed
him before men and those who denied him,[12] and his
calling down of woe upon the cities which had not
responded to his ministrations[13] all suggest a consciousness of peculiar significance on the part of Jesus as
do also the other references to himself in such statements as "come unto me", "for my sake and the
Gospel's", "but I say unto you", "my words shall
not pass away".[14] Pointing in the same direction is
his acceptance of the confessions of Nathanael[15] and
Peter.[16]

Notice must also be taken of certain of his parables—
notably those of the wicked husbandmen[17] and of
the marriage feast[18] which, as R. S. Wallace says:
"predict not only an immediate crisis for those who
were dealing with Jesus of Nazareth in the flesh, but
also an historical process which is to follow his historical life and is to be equally decisive for generations
to come."[19] These parables show that, in the Gospels'
picture of him, Jesus was conscious of fulfilling a
peculiar mission, while the account of his temptations[20]
suggests again someone conscious of an unusual place
in the world. John Howat says in one of his sermons:

[9]Matthew 13.17 = Luke 10.24.   [10]G. S. Duncan, op. cit., p. 198.
[11]Matthew 7.24–7.   [12]Matthew 10.32–3.   [13]Matthew 11.20–4.
[14]Matthew 11.28; Mark 10.29; Matthew 5.21–44; Matthew
   24.35 = Mark 13.31 = Luke 21.33.
[15]John 1.49.   [16]Matthew 16.17.
[17]Matthew 21.33–44 = Mark 12.1–11 = Luke 20.9–18.
[18]Matthew 22.1–14; cf. Luke 14.15–24.
[19]R. S. Wallace, "The Parable and the Preacher", Scottish Journal of
   Theology, vol. II (1949), p. 16.
[20]Matthew 4.1–11 = Luke 4.1–13.

In whatever way you interpret the imagery of these temptations, you must realize that they are not the kind of temptations we have to wrestle with . . . They are . . . the particular kind of temptation that faces One beginning his life-work in the full awareness of his unique mission to mankind.[21]

It is true that we do not have in the Gospels statements identical with those which the theologians of the immediately succeeding centuries made normative for Christian confessions of the next thousand years and more. But this absence is in itself significant.

That in a document like Mark's Gospel Jesus never says explicitly that he is Son of God is a very remarkable thing; for Mark himself clearly believed Jesus was the Son of God, in some sense probably not unlike that in which Paul would have used the term. It says much for the purity in which Mark has preserved the early tradition that he has nowhere intruded upon the lips of Jesus a formula which he himself believed, nor has he given any statement which would be a general over-riding reason for the absence of such a formula and which might lead us to suspect that he had been controlled by some peculiar doctrinaire twist. We see here the richness of that consciousness of the early Church in which one like Mark could believe in Jesus as Son of God and yet could record and transmit with fidelity a tradition in which Jesus never so spoke.[22]

[21] John Howat, "Alone with the Devil", *The Expository Times*, vol. LXIII (1951–2), p. 149.
[22] James Barr, "Christ in Gospel and Creed", *Scottish Journal of Theology*, vol. VIII (1955), p. 229.

These pointers to the way in which the writers of
the Gospels attributed uniqueness to Jesus are not
all that could be mentioned. Some might bring
forward the accounts of his miracles, or even the
suggestions of his pre-existence,[23] which certainly
form part of the picture. But the introduction of
such factors here would not further our present
purpose. I do not at this stage wish to suggest that
the very nature of them shows that they are beyond
historiographical investigation—whether or not they
are is a matter to be determined. What I wish to
indicate is how firmly embedded in the New Testament
picture is the element of uniqueness.

Of this element, as of others, any assessment of
the New Testament picture must take account.

A Tentative Assessment

In this chapter an attempt has been made to cover the
thought of the last hundred years in regard to the New
Testament picture of Jesus. This has been done by
selecting the views of this period which have been
most significant, and subjecting each of them to some
criticism.[1] If any conclusion is to be stated on the
basis of our consideration of these views it is this: that
each has contributed something to our understanding
of the subject but none has proved entirely satisfactory.

This suggests that our own next task is to put
forward what we regard as a satisfactory view. We
might do this by means of a much more particularized

---

[23]e.g. G. C. Berkouwer, *The Person of Christ* (Grand Rapids: Wm.
B. Eerdmans Publishing Co., 1954), pp. 163 seqq.
[1]Another significant approach of this period—that of the demythologizers—is given separate consideration in chapter IV.

discussion than we have yet engaged in—one that would take up in turn each incident, the various ways in which it is recorded and what has been said about it, and so proceed to the construction of a picture of our own. The extent of this picture's agreement with the details recorded in the New Testament would indicate our assessment of the picture of the historical Jesus there.

But this could hardly satisfy. Even if we ourselves were content with the conclusions we reached concerning each detail (and the probability is that so detailed a picture would show itself acceptable to no one but ourselves), we should still have to face the question of what validity our construction has when judged by the principles which govern sound historiographical procedure. And until that was done, our efforts would have done little towards solving what we described in the Introduction as the core of the problem of Jesus today.

Thus we are brought back to the task which we set ourselves at the beginning: the statement of the principles involved in finding the historical Jesus. The value of this chapter lies in its disclosing what thoughtful judgments about him have influenced Christian (and some non-Christian) thinking in our day, and what questions of historiographical procedure arise. To the direct discussion of these questions we are now ready to proceed.

Before doing so, however, it may be desirable to offer, on the basis of our discussion thus far, a tentative assessment of the New Testament picture of Jesus.

In the New Testament (and in the Gospels especially) there are accounts of deeds and sayings attributed to one Jesus of Nazareth, of whose actual existence there can be no reasonable doubt. While it is difficult for the modern mind to accept as factual truth everything that is said about him there, it is equally difficult for it to be satisfied with a reconstruction of that life which can find support in the Gospels only if certain portions of them are (on no basis other than their incompatibility with the reconstruction) disregarded. This man Jesus lived in first-century Palestine, and he is described for us by people who shared certain characteristics of that *milieu* no less than he did himself. Their picture of him reflects the way in which they saw him as meeting the needs which arose in the community of which they were part, but the New Testament picture cannot be explained altogether in terms of that community.

This assessment, sound as it is in its general lines, is not the end of the matter. There still remains for each historian the task of deciding which details can be accepted as authentic and of offering some explanation of how other details came to be added. There remains also for the Christian the task of showing (to himself, to other believers and to unbelievers) on what grounds he attributes to this historical figure a uniqueness not shared by any other figure of the past.

The nature of this uniqueness will be discussed in chapter III. Here, where we are making a tentative assessment of the New Testament picture, we have to take account of an element of uniqueness which is part of that picture, but which is not to be identified with (though it is closely related to) the uniqueness which the believer affirms. The New Testament picture contains a good deal which must cause even the unbelieving reader to wonder what sort of a man Jesus was.

It is apparent, then, that the problem with which we started is not one that can be satisfactorily dealt with by such approaches to the New Testament as we have had before us. These approaches only serve to point the problem more acutely: we are still left in doubt as to how we should go about finding the historical Jesus.

II

Jesus in the Light of Historiography

IN THE LAST CHAPTER a survey was made of what
has been said in recent years concerning the picture
of Jesus in the New Testament and a tentative assessment of it was given. It was suggested that the New
Testament picture presents something of an enigma:
while it contains features which many find it hard to
accept as historical, it will not do to dismiss all of it
(or even all the features difficult of acceptance) as
having no historical basis whatever. It was suggested
finally that we are still left in doubt as to how we should
go about finding the historical Jesus.

The fact is that in the presentation of these views,
each of which was in its own way a quest of the historical Jesus, there was no real consideration of what is
meant by the "historical"; each of them displays an
assumption on this score which had a large part in
making the view what it was. The "Christ-myth"
view assumed that the important thing about being
historical is to be (or to have been) in existence. The
view of liberalism was that to be historical means to
have satisfied criteria derived from studies of a different
kind. The view of consistent eschatology considered
it to mean the satisfaction of similar criteria, but free
from the presuppositions which characterized liberal-

ism.[1] The view of Form-criticism considered what was historical about Jesus to be beyond recovery. No one of these assumptions is entirely unfounded: as we shall see, each of them has to be considered in arriving at a proper understanding of the historical. But at least part of the inadequacy of each view can be traced to a failure to examine its assumptions and in particular a failure to consider what part in establishing his particular picture of Jesus can properly be played by the historian.

This failure may seem to us a strange thing: it is not so strange when we remember that practically all thinking of the past hundred years (including the thinking of noted historians) exhibits a similar failure. In the introduction to the valuable collection he has made of the views held by many scholars on the nature of historiographical research, Fritz Stern remarks: "To many historians, especially in the nineteenth century, the thought of an explicit definition of their task may well have been repugnant, for it would necessarily have involved so much of the very thing they sought to extinguish, their own selves."[2]

It is only within the last score or so of years that the majority of professional historians have become seized with the importance of such a discussion;[3] and

[1]Schweitzer failed to "radicalize" his insight concerning these presuppositions "into a questioning of the objectivity of historical research as such . . . Nor did his insight lead him to doubt the appropriateness of the sources for the kind of chronological biography he and his predecessors tried to write . . . (He) is himself one of the last spokesmen for the nineteenth-century view of the sources." James M. Robinson, *A New Quest of the Historical Jesus*, pp. 33–4.

[2]Fritz Stern (ed.), *The Varieties of History; From Voltaire to the Present* (New York: Meridian Books Inc., 1956), p. 15.

[3]My own experience is that some teachers of history at a tertiary

it has taken the onslaught of the demythologizing controversy to awaken many Christians to it.

Whatever may have been the omissions on the part of earlier thinkers, and the reasons for them, it is clear that our own consideration can proceed no further until we have examined what we mean when we speak of the historical; and it is to such an examination (particularly as it bears upon the meaning to be attached to the term "the historical Jesus") that we now turn.

The Apparent Limits of Historiography

Canons of historiography, it is commonly assumed, allow us to say of only certain parts of the New Testament that they are true.

There has not been unanimity as to which parts are in this category. Some differences occur at what may be called the "ground level": differences about the truth of certain statements taken at their face value. For example, some historiographers consider that Jesus was born at Bethlehem of Judaea in the days of Herod the king, while others deny this; some admit that he preached in a synagogue at Capernaum and that the people threatened to kill him, while others refuse to accept all the statements made in the New Testament about this incident. There are also "second level" differences; that is, differences about statements unacceptable at their face value but which (with explanations different from those advanced in the narrative itself) may nonetheless be accounts of

level form their views on this subject as they are led into discussion of it by a Christian looking for light on the particular problem with which we are concerned in these pages.

what actually took place. The stories of Jesus' miracles of healing are cases in point: some historiographers include in the category of the "historically true" those that are patient of an interpretation compatible with the findings of modern psychosomatology, while others refuse to include these stories in any way.

Such differences affect only the boundaries enclosing each group; they do not alter the fact that there is today, among Christians as among other people, general agreement that the criteria of truth acceptable by trained historiographers can allow only parts of the New Testament picture to stand.

Let us make clear what we have in mind when we speak of a general agreement that historiography cannot accept some parts of the New Testament picture.

We are not concerned with the fact that some scholars do not accept some details of that picture. Our earlier examples of both "ground level" and "second level" differences are relevant here. This sort of disagreement among experts can arise in respect of any event of the past; indeed, much historiographical work is undertaken precisely because there *are* such points of disagreement. The declared "inability" of any historiographer to accept a fact in such cases means only that he is for his part unable to agree with those who consider that the evidence points to it; he is not declaring it to be such a fact as *no* historiographical research could establish.

Nor are we concerned with that quality of uncertainty which must attach to any historical fact by the very nature of its being related to an event which is past—an uncertainty occasioned by the historian's never being able to lay his hands upon all the desirable data, and by the absence of materials which he could submit to a "controlled experiment" in order to verify his hypothesis.[1] But this uncertainty does not prevent their stating facts which, they say, historiography has "proved".[2] Every historian is prepared to accept some facts concerning the past, and it is not the uncertainty attaching to every historical fact which leads historiographers to reject some of the details of the New Testament picture.

What we are concerned with here is the assertion that certain parts of the New Testament picture are of such a nature that historiographical science is *quite unable* to state that they are "true". These are the features in the picture which declare Jesus to have been unlike other men and to have done things which no other man can do. Historiographical science declares itself unable to say that these are "true", because their very uniqueness makes it impossible to place them in a class along with others of their kind, in which they may enjoy examination by comparison, and in terms of which they may be described.[3]

Some have roundly declared that what historiography cannot pronounce to be "true" must be "false". One who adopts such an attitude is Herbert J. Muller.

---

[1] The question whether, strictly speaking, any number of verifying experiments can remove the uncertainty which attaches even to a "scientific fact" is an interesting one, but it need not detain us here. Most people concede that it is possible to achieve a greater degree of certainty concerning what is at hand than concerning what has happened in the past.

[2] See *infra.*, pp. 111-15, concerning certainty and uncertainty in historiography.

[3] Of course, some historians would contend that there *can* be a comparison of this "uniqueness" with what zealous admirers have asserted concerning other religious leaders, or with the way in which some other men of outstanding personality have made use of the psychosomatic relationship, and so on. Such historians are in fact denying that there is uniqueness in the case of Jesus.

Scientific standards of truth are not the only possible standards, of course, but they are the necessary standards for claims to literal, factual, historical truth. They do not apply to the question whether Christ was the Son of God; they do apply to the question of just what he said and did on earth. Hence the claims of the orthodox churches not only appear contrary to fact but defy the principles on which reliable knowledge rests.[4]

Here it is concluded that whatever of truth is to be said about the historical Jesus must accord with "scientific standards of truth"; all else, whatever other sort of truth it may have (and Muller does not stop to discuss what he may mean by this suggestion) cannot be "literal, factual, historical truth". Later[5] we shall consider more carefully what sort of truth can be asserted in respect of historiographical findings; here we are noting what may follow from the assertion that historiography is unable to say of certain features of the New Testament picture of Jesus that they are true.

To conclude in this way that what is beyond the criteria of historiography cannot be historically true is to reject out of hand any claim that Jesus is a unique historical figure. It is the attitude adopted by atheists, agnostics and non-Christians generally. And, indeed, once this claim has been rejected, there is little reason to enquire further concerning these "historiographically non-provable" features in the picture: they are simply dismissed, on the evidence of their own nature, as having been wrongly intruded upon it.

[4]Herbert J. Muller, *The Uses of the Past; Profiles of Former Societies* (New York: Oxford University Press, 1952), pp. 76-7.
[5]*infra*, pp. 84-6, 111-15.

A similar attitude underlies the picture of Jesus presented by the liberal school of Christian thought. In this case, too, there is ready acceptance of the claim that historiographical science has found some details of the New Testament picture unacceptable, and that what is unacceptable to modern historiography is false. Where the exponents of liberal theology differ from those who are avowedly not Christian believers is in their readiness to ascribe some sort of uniqueness to Jesus (even if only as *primus inter pares*), and their evident desire to be his followers making known everywhere what they consider to be the truth concerning him. These features undoubtedly differentiate the liberal theologian from the atheist and the agnostic, but he shares with them the same presuppositions in historiography.

The validity of these presuppositions rather than certain others (which could lead the historian to different conclusions concerning the New Testament picture) is a matter to which we must give some attention, for the extent to which presuppositions in the historian's mind determine the facts at which he arrives in the process of historiographical investigation is not always appreciated.[6] What we may note for the present is that the Christian (even the liberal Christian in so far as he is a Christian) cannot so easily dismiss these "historiographically non-provable" details in the picture. For to account for Jesus wholly upon the level of ordinary human existence is not the way in which Christians think about Jesus: always he has been thought of by them as related in a unique way to God. The nature of this relationship need not concern us at this point; it is enough to note that

[6]See, *infra*, pp. 94-118.

Christian faith[7] (which must include some factor of relying upon Jesus as no one else can be relied upon) is bound to attribute some sort of uniqueness to him. And, though we are not here discussing the form of that uniqueness,[8] and certainly not wishing to contend that any particular feature of the New Testament picture (say, the walking on the water, the feeding of the five thousand, or the empty tomb) receives from faith a guarantee which historiography denies it, this uniqueness has often been thought of as finding expression in just those details of the picture which, it is claimed, historiography cannot say are true.

There are various ways in which this Christian conviction of a difference between Jesus and other men has been expressed; and in the next chapter we shall look at some of them. "Lordship", "fulfilment", "immediacy", "divinity": these are some of the many concepts which have been advanced to express the essential difference between Jesus and other men; and Christian literature through the centuries abounds in instances of new terms, and new interpretations of old ones, being advanced to express the uniqueness of Jesus.

It is not the least of our debts to the quest of the historical Jesus upon which so much thought has been lavished that we have become profoundly convinced concerning the real humanity of Jesus. While such a conviction seems to be at one with the main stream of the Christian tradition, it has been accompanied in our day by a feeling that his true humanity (that is, his being a historical person) is impugned if at the same

[7]Some discussion of the nature of faith is entered into later. See infra, pp. 147-65.
[8]This is referred to, infra, pp. 122-40.

time it is said that Jesus was divine (or whatever other term is used to point to the uniqueness of which we have been speaking).

Christian thought has been loath to let go either the humanity which historiography has helped it to know and appreciate or the divinity which faith attests; and there has arisen the practice of contending that, while historiography cannot say that certain parts of the New Testament picture of Jesus are true, neither can it say that they are false.

So, for example, writes Herbert Butterfield: "If any man were to say that history had scientifically established or scientifically disproved the divinity of Christ, he would . . . be guilty of that intellectual arrogance which works in all the sciences as each of them transgresses its bounds in order to gain an usurped authority."[9]

The idea that there are some parts of the New Testament picture concerning which historiography is unable to say whether they are true or false has led to the suggestion that they belong to history, but to history of a different kind from that wherein historiographical criteria are relevant: namely, to something called "super-history" or "meta-history", or even "non-historical history" (*unhistorische Geschichte*) which, Barth says, every history is "in its immediacy to God . . . , i.e., it cannot be deduced and compared and therefore comprehended. But this does not mean that it ceases to be genuine history."[10]

[9]Herbert Butterfield, *Christianity and History* (London: G. Bell & Sons Ltd., 1949) pp. 18–19. Later, however, Butterfield suggests that this sort of statement can become "effective for those who have carried the narrative to intimate regions inside themselves" (*ibid.*, p. 107).
[10]Karl Barth, *The Doctrine of Creation*, Part 1, trans. J. W. Edwards,

It is not easy to say when this idea of a different sort of history arose and even less easy to trace the origin of the terms which are now in common use. Richard R. Niebuhr gives the idea an earlier planting than most other scholars when he attributes it to Immanuel Kant.[11] Whereas Kant made a distinction (though not a division) between the practical reason and the theoretical reason, declaring that some things, not to be denied, can be discerned by the former though not by the latter, this way of describing the uniqueness of Jesus speaks of a sort of history divorced from ordinary history, declaring that his uniqueness, or divinity, is discernible by those who have knowledge of *Heilsgeschichte* though not by those whose knowledge is confined to *Weltgeschichte*.[12] Niebuhr goes on to say:

> The fact that "history" or some synonym is still used to describe this level of knowledge and experience does not obviate the truth that history and nature are transcended in principle . . . The sum of the matter can be put in a few words. History and the historical self have been "naturalized", and it has become necessary to posit a

---

et. al. (vol. III. 1 of *Church Dogmatics*; Edinburgh: T. & T. Clark, 1958), p. 80.

[11]He has in mind particularly the use made of it by Karl Barth, Emil Brunner and John Knox.

[12]Richard R. Niebuhr, *Resurrection and Historical Reason* (New York: Charles Scribner's Sons, 1957), pp. 40, 59, 74, 111. Niebuhr appears to underestimate the extent to which proponents of this view recognize a conjunction of the two sorts of history. As Löwith puts it, *Weltgeschichte* and *Heilsgeschichte* "are opposite principles of two different patterns of knowledge. This difference does not exclude, but rather implies, the question of their relation." Karl Löwith, *Meaning in History; the Theological Implications of the Philosophy of History* (Chicago: University of Chicago Press 1949), p. 225.

supra-natural, supra-historical self or ego. From the perspective of the long conflict between natural science and Christian faith, the rise of *Heilsgeschichte* can be taken as simply one more landmark in the history of the triumph of science.[13]

It will be maintained in the remaining pages of this chapter, and in the next, that to concede such a "triumph" to "science" is to misunderstand the true nature of historiography and that the conviction held by Christians generally (including those who wrote the books of the New Testament) that the "divinity" is one with the "humanity" in being disclosed in the historical Jesus (or, in other words, that the "super-historical" is one with the "historical"; or, again, that the uniqueness of Jesus is part of his being a historical person) is sound.

The Historical

The Greek ἱστορία (derived from ἵστωρ "acquainted with", "one who knows") denoted knowledge obtained as the result of enquiry, or the narration of such knowledge. Thus a "history" could be an account of knowledge about any subject: Aristotle's *History of Animals* and Theophrastus' *History of Plants* were simply accounts of what was known about these things. But the word, save for some qualified and specialized usages (such as "natural history"), has long been accorded a narrower connotation. Herodotus used it as the title of a book which discussed the rise of Greece and Persia and their wars, along with a good deal of other information

[13]*op. cit.*, p. 116.

about them; and it is due as much to his usage of the word as to the principles and methodology which he pioneered that he deserves to be called the father of history.

These early connotations of the word have anticipated what may be meant when we today use the word "historical". At least three possible meanings suggest themselves.

The word "historical" may denote everything which has happened: primeval earthquakes, volcanic eruptions, battles, squabbles, contracts, marriages, riots, pillow-fights, voyages, horse-races. All happenings on this view fall within the sphere of the "historical", though in fact many will never be known by any historian—either because no one ever knew about them or because those who did left no record of their having taken place.

Actually, so broad a connotation is rarely, and then only for the sake of definition, given to the term. In all intelligent discussion it is limited in one or both of two ways. These limitations provide the second and third possible meanings of the term.

But certain ideas involved in this understanding of the term "historical" are of great value, and must be retained in any use of it.

The notion of the historical as covering "*everything* that has happened" constitutes a reminder of the incompleteness of human knowledge. It is salutary for the historian to reflect that, even if he could take into his mind everything that has been known by everybody, his knowledge must still fall short of all that has taken place. It is of greater practical import for him to remember, as he considers any section of the past, that there is more to be discovered than all his studies have at any time enabled him to see. There is a past which is a real past (and therefore "historical", in this first sense of the word) irrespective of anyone's knowing about it; and its reality stands in judgment upon all our attempts to know about it.

The notion of the historical as covering "everything that has *happened*" distinguishes it from the legendary and the mythological.[1] Legends and myths often tell us a good deal about the people among whom they arose and about those who transmitted them to succeeding generations. They may thus be data for learning about these people, but the conclusion that legends and myths are not accounts of what actually happened precludes their contents from what is "historical".

We have said that the term "historical" rarely carries the broad connotation we have just considered, and that it is usually limited in one or both of two ways. The first of these is to regard it as denoting only what has happened to mankind. We would do better, writes John Macquarrie, "to restrict the word 'history' to that period of time in which man has been active and to use some such word as 'process' for those

---

[1] A legend (Latin *legenda* "things to be read") meant originally a saint's life, or even a portion of Scripture, which was read aloud on certain occasions; it then came to include other stories (usually of a marvellous kind), and finally to denote a traditional tale without proper relationship to events.

A myth (Greek μῦθος, "something delivered by word of mouth") meant originally any subject of conversation; it then came to mean a story, especially one of doubtful authenticity; and finally to denote a legend which embodies religious beliefs. For some other connotations of "myth" see H. Butterfield, *Christianity and History*, p. 81, and H. P. Owen, *Revelation and Existence* (Cardiff: University of Wales Press, 1957), pp. 151–3. The special connotation given to the word by the demythologizers is discussed *infra*, pp. 178–83.

natural occurrences in which man has no part."[2]
Roger Shinn makes a similar distinction when he says:
"Natural history—the story of the geological development of the earth or the evolution of primates—is not
the same as human history . . . One visits the Museum
of Natural History and the Metropolitan Museum of
Art with differing expectations."[3]

Another who limits "history" in this first way is
R. G. Collingwood who refers to it as "the science of
res gestae, the attempt to answer questions about
human actions done in the past."[4] History is "humanistic, or asks questions about things done by men at
determinate times in the past", and it "ministers to
man's knowledge of man."[5] His reason for this
limitation of historical knowledge to human affairs
is that the historian's concern is for more than simply
the "outside" of events; he has a concern for the
"inside" of them too.

> By the outside of an event I mean everything
> belonging to it which can be described in terms
> of bodies and their movements: the passage of
> Caesar, accompanied by certain men, across a
> river called the Rubicon at one date, or the
> spilling of his blood on the floor of the senate-
> house at another. By the inside of an event I mean
> that in it which can only be described in thought:
> Caesar's defiance of Republican law, or the clash
> of constitutional policy between himself and his

[2]John Macquarrie, *The Scope of Demythologizing* (London: S.C.M. Press Ltd., 1960), p. 59.
[3]Roger Lincoln Shinn, *Christianity and the Problem of History* (New York: Scribner's, 1953), p. 194.
[4]R. G. Collingwood, *The Idea of History* (London: Oxford University Press, 1946), p. 9.
[5]*ibid.*, pp. 18, 19.

assassins. The historian is never concerned with either of these to the exclusion of the other. He is investigating not mere events (where by a mere event I mean one which has only an outside and no inside) but actions, and an action is the unity of the outside and inside of an event. He is interested in the crossing of the Rubicon only in its relation to Republican law, and in the spilling of Caesar's blood only in its relation to a constitutional conflict. His work may begin by discovering the outside of an event, but it can never end there; he must always remember that the event was an action, and that his main task is to think himself into this action, to discern the thought of its agent.[6]

If history is thus concerned with thought, it is clear that only human affairs can be the subject of historical knowledge, since man is "the only animal that thinks, or thinks enough, and clearly enough, to render his actions the expressions of his thoughts."[7]

Collingwood goes on to say that not all human actions are subject-matter for history and excludes conduct which is determined by natural impulses and appetites.

The historian is not interested in the fact that men eat and sleep and make love and thus satisfy their natural appetites; but he is interested in the social customs which they create by their thought

---

[6]*ibid.*, p. 213. Bultmann makes the same point concerning the insufficiency of history seen only "as a field of such events as can be fixed in time and space" by pointing out that "single events are not without connection but are connected by the chain of cause and effect", and that "such connection presupposes powers at work in the historical process"—namely, human impulses and passions. Rudolf Bultmann, *History and Eschatology* (New York: Harper & Row, 1957), p. 116.

[7]Collingwood, *op. cit.*, p. 216.

as a framework within which these appetites find
satisfaction in ways sanctioned by convention
and morality.[8]

At some points (as when he asserts that a biography,
"however much history it contains, is constructed on
principles that are not only non-historical but anti-
historical"[9]) Collingwood has over-stated his thesis,
but it is in essence a sound one. The limitation of the
historical to "everything which has happened to
mankind" need not restrict its reference to only those
events for which men are themselves responsible; it
may include reference to other events, even events in
the natural world, which have had some effect upon
mankind (or as Collingwood would probably say, have
led men by their thought to create a framework within
which they perform their actions).

We can therefore accept this as a proper limitation.
Indeed it is an inevitable one, for events which have
had some effect upon mankind are the only ones of
which knowledge is possible.

But the introduction here of the notion of "knowledge" of what has happened leads us into the second
limitation and so to the third possible meaning of the
word "historical".

The word "historical" may denote everything which
has happened of which there is knowledge.

A. D. Foster says:

History is not factuality *per se*, but *factuality*

[8]*ibid.*, p. 216.
[9]*ibid.*, p. 304. Cf. Bultmann, who justifies autobiography (and
    presumably biography generally) on the grounds that "person-
    ality experiences its own history . . . which has its own meaning"
    and that "history is also moved by the personal self-under-
    standing of the persons who are acting in history" (*op. cit.*,
    pp. 146–7).

grasped and recollected. Thus when we speak of the "dawn of history", we do not mean the beginning of temporal process, nor of the human race, but rather the earliest events which can still be reconstructed. And when we say that someone will 'go down in history', we do not simply assert that he has lived, but that he will be remembered.[10]

This may appear, like the one which determined our second meaning of "historical", an inevitable limitation. It is so in one sense, for we cannot speak intelligibly about a past of which no one knows anything. But it is a dangerous limitation if it encourages a smug acceptance of what is known now as constituting the whole of the past, or all of it that is worth knowing. The danger is all the greater if "what is known now" is taken to mean what is known by any particular historian. Here it is valuable to recall our earlier discussion of the historical as denoting *"everything that has happened"*.

Involved in this conception of the historical as what is known is the matter of judgment by the historian for, notwithstanding the evidence presented, he cannot say of anything which he considers intrinsically impossible, or even very unlikely, that he "knows" that it happened. Knowledge is not a faculty operating in a compartment sealed off from the rest of a man; his knowledge plays a part in making any man what he is, and what a man is plays a part in determining what he will accept as knowledge. When therefore we say

[10]Andrew Durwood Foster Jr., "The Theological Problem of the 'Jesus of History' and the 'Christ of Faith': A Critical and Constructive Analysis Especially in the Light of Some Leading Thinkers of the Nineteenth Century" (unpublished Doctor's thesis, Union Theological Seminary, New York, 1956), p. 50.

that the historical denotes everything which has happened of which there is knowledge we are saying that as far as any particular historian is concerned, what is historical (that is, what he knows to have happened) is affected in some way by a judgment he himself makes. To this we shall have occasion to return.[11]

Also involved in this conception of the historical as what is known is the matter of significance. What is known by any historian is determined by his interest as well as by the evidence that is available to him; and both these factors presuppose a decision by someone as to significance. Thus when Seeley used to insist that "the history of the Staffordshire Potteries was *not* history" this was because, as Rowse remarks, "he was only interested really in the life of the state, and the conflict of power between states."[12] He had made a decision as to what was significant and on the basis of that decision had removed certain interests from the realm of the historical.

From this discussion concerning possible meanings of the term "historical", we can proceed to an indication of what we mean when we speak of "the historical Jesus".

We mean by this, in the first place, all the things that took place in the life of Jesus: what he said and did, whether or not we today know, or can know, about them. And, irrespective of any assertion made by historiographers, however skilled, such things as the miracles and the Resurrection, if they actually took place, are "historical" in this sense.

[11]*infra.* pp. 115-18.
[12]A. L. Rowse, *The Use of History* (London: Hodder & Stoughton Ltd., 1946), p. 62.

Secondly, although this first meaning is a reminder that we may yet discover other things about Jesus, we must say that we mean by the "historical Jesus" only what in fact is known about him. And what is known about him is confined almost entirely to what is said of him in the writings which have been included in the New Testament.[13] Thus "the historical Jesus" and "the picture of Jesus in the New Testament" seem to be synonymous.

But thirdly, as we have already noted (and have asserted to be the core of the problem we are discussing), some are not prepared to accept the whole New Testament picture as historical; and so there is brought into the meaning of the term "historical" the factor of judgment by present-day historians.

Generally speaking, the picture of Jesus which any historian has is the New Testament picture minus whatever that historian finds himself unable to accept. In his rejection of certain parts of the New Testament picture he exercises a judgment of his own; and it may be added that his removal of anything from that picture is related to his bringing of something to it.

Whether any such judgment on the part of the historian is justified stands as a vital question; and our answer to it will emerge as we consider what is involved in knowledge of the past. We shall observe first how that knowledge differs from scientific knowledge (as that is commonly understood[14]) and secondly, what part the historian himself plays in arriving at it.[15] Our treatment of these is occasioned by the *milieu* in

---

[13]What little knowledge of Jesus we may gain from sources outside the New Testament is referred to *supra*, pp. 11-13. It corroborates, rather than extends, what is known from the New Testament.
[14]*infra*, pp. 86-92.   [15]*infra*, pp. 94-118

which thoughtful people find themselves at the present time, and points to tendencies in which historians are prone to be misled.

Historiography and Natural Science

The last century and a half have seen tremendous progress in the acquirement of knowledge about the physical world, and every moment in the life of a civilized man sees him surrounded by, and dependent upon the results of this knowledge. It is small wonder that "science"[1] should be held in such high regard, and that the kind of thinking responsible for such progress should have been extended to other fields. In this way arose positivism which, Collingwood says, "may be defined as philosophy acting in the service of natural science, as in the Middle Ages philosophy acted in the service of theology."[2]

This manner of thinking was not without its influence upon historians, and there arose a generation who, like J. B. Bury, considered "history" (historiography, in our terminology) to be "a science, no less and no more"[3] and who, adopting as a battle-cry Leopold von Ranke's statement, *wie es eigentlich gewesen,*[4]

[1]"There is a slang usage, like that for which 'hall' means a music-hall or 'pictures' moving pictures, according to which 'science' means natural science". Collingwood, *op. cit.,* p. 249.

[2]*ibid.,* p. 126.

[3]"The Science of History", his Inaugural Lecture when in 1902 he succeeded Lord Acton as Regius Professor of Modern History at Cambridge. The Lecture is printed in Fritz Stern (ed.) *The Varieties of History,* pp. 210–23.

[4]This phrase occurs in the Preface to his *Histories of the Latin and Germanic Nations from* 1494–1514, which Stern has translated and included in his *op. cit.* pp. 55–8. Stern points out that "Ranke meant this now famous phrase as a modest self-denial, feeling that history ought no longer to play the role of philosopher or

patterned their historiography along a line which showed clearly the source of inspiration.

Rowse says:

It is easy to see what the main influences were that made academic historians insist upon the scientific character of their subject. There was the increasing insistence of a scientific age upon exactness, accuracy, objectivity; . . . most important of all there was the immense and deserved, if somewhat disproportionate, prestige of the physical sciences with their astounding achievements in theory and practice to their credit.[5]

And Muller:

Historians of the last century were striving to make their subject intellectually respectable in an age of science . . . They had to combat the common tendencies to entertain and edify, to exploit the dramatic and spectacular, to teach political and religious lessons, or to leap to grandiose philosophies of history. These tendencies are still so popular that we can scarcely afford to ridicule any aspiration to objectivity and exactitude.[6]

The striving after objectivity characteristic of the modern scientific method, its continual questioning of the data and of the statements made on the basis of them, its endeavour to present for acceptance only what can be publicly appreciated, its discounting of any notion of esoteric knowledge: all these are part of the pattern of historiography today, and are features

---

judge; only later was it taken as a boast, as if history could in fact achieve this kind of exactitude" (*ibid.*, p. 16).
[5]Rowse, *op. cit.*, p. 91.   [6]Muller, *op. cit.*, p. 28.

which mark off its results from what were accepted as historical conclusions in earlier centuries. They have helped to make historiography a means of acquiring knowledge able to stand with respect among the learned.

It is fruitless to spend time discussing whether this particular means of acquiring knowledge is rightly to be designated a "science". As Morris Cohen points out, the quarrel on this score "has been largely verbal, more concerned with maintaining or rejecting the prestige that the word 'science' carries nowadays than with the precise meaning of the question."[7] What cannot be gainsaid is that the respect accorded to "science" has resulted in a general tendency to assess historiographical findings not only by the extent to which they are compatible with the findings of natural science, but also by the extent to which the method of arriving at them corresponds to natural science's methodology.

It should be noted, therefore, that historiography is different from natural science in three important ways.[8]

(a) While natural science ideally has its object immediately present, it is of the very nature of historiography not to have its object immediately present.

The microscope, the balance, the crucible—these symbols of the way in which natural science goes about

[7]Morris R. Cohen, *The Meaning of Human History* (La Salle, Illinois: The Open Court Publishing Co., 1947), p. 36.

[8]It is recognized that the "natural science" referred to here proceeds on assumptions which are now called into question by scientists themselves. (For instance, studies in relativity would deny the "timelessness" of natural science to which attention is drawn on p. 88). Nonetheless the concepts here denoted as those of natural science carry a great deal of weight in contemporary assessments of soundness in historiographical procedure. See also *infra*, pp. 92-3.

its work—all presuppose the presence of objects upon which they can be used, and the possibility of the objects being examined in a way designed to elicit particular information. Natural science moves forward on just such carefully directed examination of what it has before it. Not so with historiography, which is concerned precisely with that which is no more, and the traces of which often refuse in the most tantalizing manner to tell the historian the thing that he is most interested in knowing.

All historians will accept the statement of Keatinge on this point:

> In history, as opposed to natural science, the fact which is at hand for observation is not the historical fact, but merely a description of it, and in many, if not in most cases, a very unreliable one. The transition from the document to the fact is difficult, occupies a great part of the historian's time, and dictates to him the nature of his method. In history there is thus an additional, and frequently a very uncertain step, which is not to be found to the same extent in natural science.[9]

Henri Pirenne puts the matter more picturesquely when he says that the materials with which the historian works

> are merely the vestiges of events and not even authentic vestiges. One might compare them with foot-prints in the sand which wind and rain have half-effaced. To reproduce even an approximation of this picture, arduous and minute work is indispensable.[10]

[9]Cited by Rowse (who gives no reference), *op. cit.*, p. 183.
[10]"What Are Historians Trying to Do?", in *Methods in Social Science, A Case Book*, edited by Stuart Rice, Committee on Scientific

(b) While natural science ideally is concerned with classes, it is of the very nature of historiography to be concerned with the unique.

If natural science is to do its work properly there are a *number* of objects to be submitted to the microscope, the balance and the crucible: and it is on the basis of examining many such objects that the scientist declares what, under certain conditions, all the objects of a class will do. The "controlled experiment", basic to the pursuit of natural science, is one which can be repeated again and again. But the historian cannot call up such conditions for conducting his enquiry; he can nowhere find other occurrences of the same event, and can never manufacture such conditions as will enable the event to take place again. The concern of historiography is with the unique.[11]

This feature of concern with the unique draws attention to three factors indispensable to the search for knowledge of the past; each of them distinguishes the work of historiography from that of natural science.

There is, first, the factor of time. The ingredients of a compound under scientific examination are, it is true, affected in certain ways by what has happened to them in the past but, given the same ingredients at any time, the same compound will result. There is

---

Method in the Social Sciences of the Social Science Research Council (Chicago: University of Chicago Press, 1931), p. 438, cited by C. S. Urban, *An Analysis of History and Historical Writing* Park College Press, 1955), pp. 16–17.

[11]Historians do, from time to time, put events into a "class" if they find this convenient for the selection and "classification" of their material; and they do make use of what they believe to have taken place on some other occasions in arriving at their conclusions concerning what took place on a particular occasion. But this does not affect the essential uniqueness of each event.

thus a timelessness about the objects of natural science which cannot be predicated of those with which historiography has to do. As M. C. D'Arcy remarks, "the scientist wants to discover what happens *whenever p*, the historian what happened *when p.*"[12]

Secondly, there persists in all historiographical enquiry the factor of inexplicability. Morris Cohen writes:

> In history, as in biology, we need the concept of the "sport", that is, the extreme variation, the course of whose varying we do not know and cannot find out, since all we can find are repeatable patterns and such repeatable patterns cannot explain extreme variation. The difference, however, is that in biology we can more or less point out the normal from which the sport is a variant, whereas in history it is hard to say just what the normal is, and uniquenesses are much more common even than in the realm of biology where one frequently hears the remark that no two living things are exactly alike.[13]

Whether or not it is true, as Toynbee suggests, that "the play of Intellect and Will is the only movement known to Man that appears to be unquestionably non-recurrent",[14] there can be no doubt that the part which human decisions play in the making of history confronts historiography with issues absent from other forms of enquiry. As Trevelyan says:

> Men are too complicated, too spiritual, too various, for scientific analysis; and the life

[12]M. C. D'Arcy, *The Sense of History* (London: Faber & Faber Ltd., 1959), p. 22.
[13]Morris R. Cohen, *op. cit.*, p. 112.
[14]Arnold Toynbee, *An Historian's Approach to Religion* (London: Oxford University Press, 1956), p. 10.

history of millions cannot be inferred from the
history of single men. History, in fact, is more a
matter of rough guessing from all the available
facts. And it deals with intellectual and spiritual
forces which cannot be subjected to any analysis
that can properly be called scientific.[15]

And Butterfield:

To survey history requires great elasticity of
mind because the processes involved are infinitely
more supple and flexible than people imagine
who make pictorial diagrams borrowed from
biology or other sciences, or are deceived by some
pattern in text-book abridgements, so that they
look for something to which human personalities
are only the means.[16]

In the third place, the concern of historiography
with the unique involves the factor of possibility. Its
concern with the unique, the unrepeatable, means that
historiography cannot say with absolute certainty[17]
what took place on a particular occasion. It also means
that it cannot say with absolute certainty what *could
not possibly* have taken place.

So to speak of each event as unique, and of its being
impossible to make absolute pronouncements about it,
does not mean that the historian must allow that
anything at all could have happened, and adopt a
naively credulous attitude concerning every assertion
that is made. He has the right, and indeed the duty
to assume what must be assumed in all searching for
knowledge: that some things remain constant, and
that, for instance, so-called "laws of nature" did not

---

[15]Cited by Rowse (who gives no reference), *op. cit.*, p. 92.
[16]Herbert Butterfield, *Christianity and History*, p. 67.
[7]On the "certainty" of historical knowledge, see *infra*, pp. 111-15.

come into operation only yesterday. Thus, as Foster says,

> the critical historian is prejudiced when he confronts the question, say, of whether the mountain really did go to Mohammed. But he is only prejudiced by that scientific conceptuality which defines the bare possibility of critical knowledge.[18]

And, according to Urban, Richard von Mises dramatizes this factor of internal criticism, disclosing (unintentional) distortion of the facts

> when he asserts that even if all witnesses agreed that they saw an important statue shake its head on a particularly solemn occasion, this testimony would be disallowed by the historian. Such judgment would be the result of the past experience of the historian, including his knowledge of the behaviour of both statues and crowds.[19]

What must nonetheless be recognized is that, in the last analysis, "that scientific conceptuality which defines the bare possibility of critical knowledge", and "the past experience of the historian" are themselves matters upon which it would be presumptuous to make absolute pronouncements. One result of the critical historian's investigations may be the disclosure that these things have been incomplete.

(c) While natural science ideally does not pass judgments, it is of the very nature of historiography to pass judgments.

The aim of natural science is to let the facts speak for themselves: to examine its objects and to note

---

[18]Foster, *op. cit.*, p. 67.

[19]Urban, *op. cit.*, p. 18, referring to Richard von Mises, *Positivism, A Study in Human Understanding* (Cambridge: Harvard University Press, 1951), p. 22.

exactly what information they provide, to allow nothing of the scientist's personality and preferences to intrude upon his record of what the objective facts disclose. For historiography, however, this is not so: its aim is to present a picture of the past which has more in it than a mere noting of things which have taken place.

It is along this line that Urban distinguishes history from annals and from chronicle. History, he says, is not annals, for history is retrospective whereas annals "were a sort of primitive journalism of the then present"; and history is not chronicle, for history "must possess an order beyond mere succession in time."[20] Fulton Sheen points out that "science is only a record of what is happening, whereas history is a record of what matters."[21]

All this implies judgment, not impersonal narration. The claim of utter impersonality, Muller says, "implied that the significance of human history was to be discovered by systematic avoidance of significant generalization or judgment. It was based, Carl Becker remarked, on the strange philosophical assumption that by not taking thought a historian could add a cubit to his stature."[22]

And one of the explicit assumptions from which Muller proceeds is that the force of human will "makes it necessary to pass ethical judgments on history, and that such judgments are in fact implicit in the works of the most resolutely amoral historians."[23]

It would be wrong to leave this discussion of the difference between natural science and historiography

[20]Urban, op. cit., p. 6.
[21]Fulton Sheen, Philosophy of Religion (New York: Appleton-Century-Crofts, 1948), p. 250; cited by Shinn, op. cit., p. 165.
[22]Muller, op. cit., p. 28.   [23]ibid., p. 30.

without noticing that natural science does not always operate in the ways that have been suggested: it was for this reason that the word "ideally" was inserted. What actually happens is that the ideal suggested in (a) is always, that in (b) almost always, and that in (c) only sometimes, attained.

It is to be noted also that there is a growing tendency for scientists, recognizing that what was once regarded as the ideal is not attainable, to adopt an amended conception of their discipline. This may be due in part, as Muller and Shinn seem to think,[24] to their taking over certain of the principles of historiography. A much more potent influence has been the out-working of what was from the outset a highly commendable feature of the scientific method: namely, its readiness to question and correct all preconceptions, including its own. In any case, what we have as the *credo* of scientists these days includes a recognition of the limited and fallible nature of their own conclusions, as well as of factors of present interest and personal inclination which influence the way in which those conclusions are sought and presented. In these circumstances, much of what we have presented as "of the very nature of historiography" should be recognized as being "of the very nature of natural science" also.

Yet it is the earlier, more rigid, understanding (the one we have presented, somewhat anachronistically, as its "ideal") of natural science which most people have in mind when they attack or defend it—particularly when they are contending *vis-à-vis* the claims of religion. Certainly it is this notion which we wish to prevent from dominating our thinking about the past;

[24]Muller, *op. cit.*, p. 280. Shinn, *op. cit.*, p. 196.

in so far as natural science itself has withdrawn from this notion, the position advanced in these pages is strengthened.

Historiography and the Historian

In considering what is involved in knowledge of the past we have discussed the relationship between historiography and natural science. We now take up the relationship between historiography and the historian for in connection with this matter too there is at the present time a good deal of misunderstanding.

What is to be made plain is that appreciation of the historical must take account of the part played by the historian. (There can of course be no knowledge of the past without a historian.)

1. *The historian plays a part in determining what is significant.* Earlier in our discussion we noticed three possible meanings of the word "historical".[1] We need here to remind ourselves of two:[2] the word may mean all that has happened in the past (whether anyone knows about it or not) or it may mean that portion of what has happened in the past of which there is knowledge. We saw then that to assume that these two things are the same would end all possibility of progress in historiography.[3]

If we ask how it comes about that there are past events of which there is no knowledge (events therefore which are "historical" in the one sense and not in the

[1]*supra*, pp. 76-82.
[2]The third meaning (which limited "historical" to what has happened to mankind) is not significant for our discussion here.
[3]There might remain the tasks of committing what is known to writing and of passing it on to others.

other), three possible answers suggest themselves. It may be that these events were never by anyone judged significant enough for data concerning them to be recorded in any form at all. It may be that though they were once considered significant (and might still be considered so if we knew enough about them), material for a historian to work on is no longer available. A third possibility is that despite the availability of material no one has deemed their subject-matter worthy of investigation.

These answers show how intimately related are knowledge of an event and its significance. The fact is that to be historical (in any sense of the word relevant here where we are considering the nature of *knowledge* of the past) is to be significant. If it were not so there would be no incentive[4] for, and no means of historical knowledge.

What can be meant when we talk about the "significance" of any happening?

There are many instances of the thing which seems of greatest significance to one historian, or group of historians, being discounted by others as quite insignificant; moreover, what has great significance from one point of view may be considered by the same historian looking at it from another point of view, or at some other time, to have little or none.

An amusing example of the first of these classes is given by R. L. P. Milburn. He refers to the well-known story of the foreign potentate on a visit to London, who, being entertained to a classical concert, was found to have derived greatest enjoyment from

---

[4]Incentive is a prerequisite for acquiring historical knowledge. Cf. Shinn: "The significance of a fact is often known before the fact is verified", *op. cit.*, p. 6.

the tuning-up of the instrumentalists. The point, Milburn says, is this:

> No doubt the English musical critics wrote, each to his own paper, a learned and correct appreciation of the concert; but one may be sure that not even the fullest account would even have referred to the squeaks and scrapings which preceded the appearance of the conductor. Yet, if the Shah had been required to do the reporting, *his* education and perceptions would have impelled him to use up his column in a description of those—to us—random irrelevances, to which the Brahms and the Schubert were, in his view, but a tedious epilogue.[5]

This illustrates our first point: what seems of greatest significance to one seems quite insignificant to others. And if we add something to Milburn's account, we can illustrate our second point from the same incident. The one thing which all (including, presumably, the English musical critics) remember about this occasion is that the visiting dignitary was more impressed with the tuning-up than with anything else; and so what was once considered of no consequence is now, by the same people, considered to be the one thing worth relating.

The fact seems to be that a judgment made concerning significance must be a partial judgment: others may disagree with it and the historian himself may amend it. Any attempt to discern objective criteria for the measurement of significance is not likely to be successful.

Morris Cohen suggests that

[5]R. L. P. Milburn, *Early Christian Interpretations of History* (London: Adam and Charles Black, 1954), p. 13.

the question of relative importance might conceivably be regarded from the point of view of what is more fundamental in explanation. If war and politics could not explain the art, science and literature of the Greeks, while the culture consisting of these elements could explain the military and political events, the more primary elements would, for logical purposes, be the more important.[6]

But he finds it necessary to add immediately: "It would, however, be difficult to prove that this is the case." The chain of causation[7] may for all we know run through all history, but any attempt to discern its every link and then put it with others in proper order is bound to end in frustration; means do not exist for the correction of whatever formulae are put forward by different historians.

The criterion of measured effect might be put forward with greater hope of general acceptance.

Is there any objective principle or criterion according to which we can decide which of two facts is more important? The answer is clear in regard to any determinable factor of which we can have more or less. Thus one fact is more important than another if it affects more people for a longer time or in a measureably more intense manner. The fact that such importance varies with time by no means denies its objectivity.[8]

But to say so much is to say very little for we have no certain ways of measuring the spread, or intensity,

[6]Morris R. Cohen, *op. cit.*, p. 227.
[7]The distinction which Cohen draws between causation and correlation is a useful one; *op. cit.*, chapter 4 *passim*.
[8]Morris R. Cohen, *op. cit.*, p. 226.

of what affects people. And in the last sentence
Cohen appears to have confused "importance" with
"a judgment concerning importance". If either of
these has "objectivity", it must be the former; it is
the latter, as experience tells us, which "varies with
time".

If there is anything to be said concerning the
objective measurement of significance it is this: what
is significant is what many people want, or need, to
know about; what many people want, or need, to
know about (in other words, what usually finds its
way into history books) is what affects, or could affect,
many people;[9] and such objectivity as statements on
these matters have is given them by the consensus of
historians' opinions. But consensus of opinion is not
always a sure guide to truth, and each historian plays
his own part in determining what is significant.

Our understanding of this part will be furthered if
we recognize that a judgment concerning significance
can only be made after the event.

It is in the light of what is seen to have followed
from it that an event is said to be significant. Nothing
in the youthful Gavrilo Princip's shooting of Franz
Ferdinand in 1914, considered in itself, shows it to be
more significant than the slaying of any one man by
another; its significance is due to the train of events
which it touched off. No one is really born great; it
is because of subsequent happenings that the circumstances of this or that person's birth are considered
worth noting. This sort of thing has to be said concerning every "significant event" in history: it is

[9]There might be added to this the criterion of having consequences
over a long period of time. But this would suggest that the longer
the time that has elapsed since an event took place, the more
worthy it is of investigation.

seen to be significant *after* it has happened. If indeed a contemporary event is said to be a significant one, this is an interim judgment based on an opinion about what will follow from it;[10] and it is often the case that what is thought at the time to be an epoch-making event is considered from the perspective of later years to be of quite minor significance, or may even pass from human memory altogether.

To say this is to say that any thought concerning the significance of an event has to include not only the event but also what may follow from it. Indeed, perhaps "what may follow" must be thought of as part of the event itself. This is the view of John Knox who considers that the question, "What was the event as an objective historical occurrence?" would be better put in this way: "What were the circumstances and incidents which together with the responses made to them and the meanings found in them constituted the event?"[11] Two quotations will make Knox's meaning clearer:

> An event is not something hypothetical and unrecoverable which lies before or behind the experience of the persons to whom and among whom it occurred; an historical event is this "something" as it was received and responded to, as it was remembered and interpreted, as it became creative in history.[12]

> All historical events occur in a social context, among or within human groups, for people and

[10]cf. the way in which, to emphasize the importance of a present, or pending, event, it is said: "History will show this to have been . . ."
[11]John Knox, *Criticism and Faith* (London: Hodder & Stoughton Ltd., 1953), p. 36.
[12]*ibid.*, p. 32.

to people; and this social context belongs to the very being of the event as such. An event without the social response to it is not an event; it does not belong to history at all.[13]

Thus the judgment concerning significance of which we have been thinking, and what Knox calls "response", appear to be closely connected, if in fact they are not to be identified. Certainly, anyone's response to an event must depend upon what significance he sees it to have. Knox, however, seems to reserve the term "response" for those who are in close chronological proximity to the event and he does not give clear expression to the fact that, so long as an event is being remembered, a response is being made to it.[14] And, since it is being remembered so long as an historian is enquiring into it, his response, on Knox's terms, is part of the event itself. As Bultmann puts it, the historian has a "life-relation" (*Lebensverhältnis*) to the matter, and it is only when the problems involved strike him as vital questions that this life-relation is genuine.[15]

That is to say, the significance of an event is related in a very real way to things that have taken place *after* it, including the activity of each historian who considers it.

---

[13]*ibid.*, p. 59.

[14]He does say, concerning "the event of which Jesus is the centre", that "like all events it is so inextricably involved in the interminable skein of history that it cannot be said to have beginning or end", *op. cit.*, p. 59. His recognition that no "event" has "beginning or end" fixed appears more clearly in his later book, *The Death of Christ* (New York: Abingdon Press, 1958), pp. 127, 131.

[15]R. Bultmann, "Ist voraussetzunglose Exegese möglich?" *Theologische Zeitschrift*, vol. XIII (1957), p. 414. See also: *History and Eschatology*, p. 113; *Jesus Christ and Mythology*, p. 50.

Some writers have gone so far as to suggest that this close association of any event with what follows means that later happenings can bring about a change in events that have already taken place. A general presentation of this point of view is made by William Temple in *Nature, Man and God*: "the future does not merely disclose in the past something which was always there, but causes the past, while retaining its own nature, actually to be, in its own organic union with its consequences, something which in isolation it neither is nor was."[16]

And John McIntyre gives a particular presentation of it when he writes:

Given a series of *a b c d* at time t_1, at which time the members of the series are problematic in character, many things may be said about them but the full significance of them cannot be grasped. Now at time t_2 appears event X, which stands to *a b c d* in the relation to them which we describe as fulfilment (f). What I am maintaining is that the fact that *a b c d* are, subsequently to their happening, found to be related to X by f actually alters their character. In this new relation in which they stand at time t_2 and in which they did not stand at time t_1, because X had not then happened, they acquire attributes which they did not have before. I do not just mean that we who live at time t_3 are now able to understand them better than men who lived between t_1 and t_2, or that we can have a view of them now which was impossible then, and that the difference is something subjective to the observers; I really do mean that there can take place qualitative changes

[16]*op. cit.*, p. 210; cited by Shinn, *op. cit.*, p. 207.

in events after they have happened, or more accurately, that the Incarnation effects this kind of change, for I am not at present concerned with the question of whether it happens in other connections.[17]

I find it impossible to accept what is plainly asserted in these statements. The clue to understanding them lies, I believe, in Temple's employment of the phrase, "in isolation", and McIntyre's of the phrases, "problematic in character", "full significance", and "fulfilment". What these writers are pointing to is the fact that an event cannot be understood without regard for what has followed, and may still follow, from it. Without taking this into consideration the event, though it "retains its own nature" and "many things may be said about it", is not what it is seen to be in the light of later events; but to describe this situation as one in which there takes place a qualitative change in the event is to misconceive the nature of the past.

What this point of view brings to light in a forceful way is the truth that no event can, at any time, be thought of as "finished"—and certainly not as "finished with". Always there is the possibility of a further response involving a new judgment concerning its significance.

This is the truth behind Bultmann's enigmatic statement:

To each historical phenomenon belongs its future, a future in which alone it will appear as that which it really is—to speak precisely we must say: the future in which it evermore appears as that which it is. For ultimately it will show itself

[17] John McIntyre, *The Christian Doctrine of History*, pp. 91–2.

in its very essence only when history has reached its end.[18]

A judgment concerning significance does not have regard only for what has followed from an event; it takes into consideration also what is seen to have led up to it.

Any event may be seen as at the beginning, or at the end, of a train of events; and that whole train may in turn be considered as an event which itself stands at the beginning or at the end of another train. We may speak of the Second World War as an event, or of the Second World War as made up of a series of events (the Battle of Britain, the Invasion of Norway, the Siege of Tobruk, the Coral Sea Battle, and so on), and, again, of each of these as a series of events (the Battle of Britain as made up of the raid on Coventry, the attack of October 1st, the shooting down of Flying Officer Smith, and so on). Or we may speak of the Second World War as one event among those which make up the event of British-German relations in the twentieth century. Any of these "events" is related to what has gone before as well as to what come after, so that an appreciation of its significance must have regard for both.

What emerges from our discussion is that any division of history into "eras", or "movements"[19] or "events" is an arbitrary business, which involves disjoining a piece of the temporal process in a way that subtracts something of its reality.

To do this is a convenient procedure and, so long as it is remembered that no event ever takes place

---

[18]Rudolf Bultmann, *History and Eschatology*, p. 120.
[19]Each of these terms can, like the term "event", be used to refer to a large or a small segment of the historical process.

without antecedents and consequents, the ends of investigation are served by it. I do not wish to suggest any other procedure as desirable or even possible: there is no other way in which enquiry into the past can be carried on. Nor do I wish, by my use of the word "arbitrary", to suggest that the historian's selection of some events rather than others to make up what he sees as an era or a movement bears no relationship to anything that is integral to the events themselves: it is the case that certain events are linked with some rather than others. The intention is to underline that any selection for any purpose is dependent to some extent upon the historian who makes it.

All this makes it very plain that the historian plays a part in determining what is significant.

2. *The historian plays a part in determining what is possible*. Michael Perry cites the example of a man by the fire with the paper, whose wife informs him that a dog is digging up his newly-planted wall-flowers. In a flash the man is out of his chair. Yet, if his wife's statement had been that there were unicorns nibbling at his plants he would continue his reading. The amount of evidence is the same in each case, says Perry; the man's acceptance of it depends upon his presuppositions.[20]

When it is said of an alleged happening in the past that it is "possible", the meaning is that the historian who makes that statement concedes that this thing could have taken place; whether it actually did is another, though of course closely related question to be answered in the light of the information that he has

[20]Michael C. Perry, "Believing and Commending the Miracles", *The Expository Times*, vol. LXXIII (1961–2), p. 340.

about it. When it is said that the alleged happening is "impossible",[21] the meaning is that the historian who makes that statement is applying criteria, not derived from the directly relevant data, to decide that however unanimous the contemporary testimony (agreement and early date being among the chief criteria respected by historians) this thing just did not take place; the question of the statue shaking its head, mentioned earlier,[22] is a case in point. What appears as an objective signification of "impossibility" is in fact what the majority of historians (or perhaps all of them) consider to be impossible. The statement that past ages have accepted what later ages have rejected (or *vice versa*) means that some historians have regarded as possible what others have regarded as impossible.

The fact that a man will, as we say, "believe anything" discounts him in the eyes of his fellows because he shows himself to be lacking in the exercise of that questioning scepticism which is prerequisite to the pursuit of all knowledge, including knowledge of the past. But there is a sense in which a man of whom it can be said that he will "*not* believe anything" is on that account to be judged a very bad historian.

3. *The historian plays a part in establishing the facts.* It will be as well to recall our distinction between "event" and "fact". The former denotes something which has happened in the past, irrespective of anyone's having knowledge of it; the latter denotes what the historian knows of something which has happened in

[21]Sometimes a historian says that a thing "could not possibly have happened", when he means only that the data cannot, in his judgment, be rightly interpreted in that way. Here "impossible" is being used as a synonym for "not supported by the evidence".
[22]*Supra,* p. 91.

the past. Thus when it is said that the historian plays a part in establishing the facts, it is not being claimed that the historian's apprehension now can work any change in what actually took place at some previous time. What the historian knows or thinks about the event is part of the "response" to it, but the notion that this can effect any change in what actually took place has already been rejected.[23] It is being said however that the historian's knowledge of the event (and so in one sense, because no event is ever really "finished",[24] the event itself) is made what it is, at least in part, by the historian himself. As we have already said in more than one connection, it is essential for the progress of historiography that the distinction between "event" and "fact" be recognized. It is also essential to recognize that the historian at any point knows only the fact, not the event.[25] And he arrives at *facts* by interpretation of *data*.[26]

What is meant by "data"[27] are the various pieces of evidence—documentary, archaeological and other—which present themselves for examination in connection with any event.

These data may come within purview from many quarters, and may include some which are under examination for a purpose other than the investigation

[23]*supra*, p. 102.   [24]*supra*, p. 102.

[25]Even if the historian tells of an event in which he himself played a part, his knowledge of it is limited to the facts he can establish.

[26]I owe this terminology to John McIntyre, who used it in his Lectures at the University of Sydney; see also his "Christ and History", *The Reformed Theological Review*, vol. VIII, no. 3 (August 1949), pp. 29–30. Similar terminology is used by Cohen, *op. cit.*, p. 44, Collingwood, *op. cit.*, pp. 222–3, 243–4, and D'Arcy, *op. cit.*, pp. 48, 52.

[27]A datum may relate to a large or a small segment of the historical process. See *supra*, pp. 102-3 the remarks concerning the use of "event".

of the particular event upon which they are seen to throw light. Thus the historian who, with a view to understanding more of the Battle of Britain, is reading the war memoirs of Winston Churchill, may come across a reference there to Halifax's refusal to lead a government from the House of Lords, and consider this of great importance in coming to a proper understanding of the British system of parliamentary government.[28] As Collingwood says: "Anything is evidence which is used as evidence, and no one can know what is going to be useful as evidence until he has had occasion to use it."[29]

Such data as are available in any case may or may not be adequate for the purpose. E. A. Judge points out that "the historian has no means of knowing how representative his data are . . . If this was a random selection, all would be well; we could assume that they were typical. But it is not."[30]

Indeed it is very rarely the case that the data available are anything like a random selection. On the contrary, their survival is often due to a process of very deliberate selection; and they are presented as already the result of someone's interpretation. Thus the historian always works in some degree of darkness concerning the soundness of the basis on which he builds.

It is this which makes me unable to agree with Judge when he writes:

A sharp distinction must be drawn between the

---

[28]Winston S. Churchill, *The Second World War*, vol. 1 (London and Melbourne: Cassell & Co. Ltd., 1948), pp. 523-4.

[29]R. G. Collingwood, *op. cit.*, p. 280.

[30]E. A. Judge, "The Times of This Ignorance; Christian Education as a Reappraisal of History", *Journal of Christian Education*, vol. 1 (1958), p. 134.

study of historical data and the study of history itself. The data of history are objects surviving from the past and facts recorded about it on good authority; they are verified, analysed and supplied to the historian by the appropriate expert, that is the archaeologist or philologist as the case may be: in this respect our knowledge of the past is of the same order as our knowledge of particular objects or events in the present. The historian himself, however, works at a different level.[31]

As I see it, there can be no assessment of data which does not call for judgment on the part of the historian,[32] and there can be ultimately *no* "distinction between the study of historical data and the study of history itself". The data are the very stuff of historiography.

Immediately any data present themselves for examination they become subject to the process of interpretation. The historian never has before him uninterpreted, certainly ascertained events; what he has are data, interpreted and being interpreted.

All the materials which the historian uses . . . are already classified, not only by the spatial and temporal categories of all experience, but also by social categories, e.g. nationality, government, peace and war, as well as by categories of importance. Without such categories intelligible discourse would be impossible, and the course of history

---

[31]*ibid.*, p. 133.

[32]cf. Marc Bloch's contention that few sciences are forced to use so many dissimilar tools at the same time and that the historian should possess at least a smattering of all the principal techniques of his trade, if only to learn the strength of his tools and the difficulty of handling them (*The Historian's Craft*, p. 68, cited in T. A. Roberts, *History and Christian Apologetic* (London: S.P.C.K., 1960), p. 27).

would either melt into an ineffable absolute of which nothing in particular could be said or else break apart into atomic facts without real connection.[33]

"Facts" are the conclusions which, from time to time, the historian draws as a result of his interpretation of the data; and the soundness of any fact established by the historian depends upon the number and appropriateness of the data which he has taken up in his interpretation, and the manner in which he has gone about interpreting them. He himself can never be satisfied about his facts while he believes that there are data which he has not considered. The assessment of his work made by others will similarly be proportionate to their estimate of the data he has considered and of the way he has interpreted them.

These facts may at any time themselves become data for further investigation, when they will be subject to the same process of interpretation as were the original data. And it is possible that any fact, when used as a datum, will be interpreted in a new way and may even be dismissed altogether. Historiography is thus a continuous process, the interpretation of data and the establishment of facts proceeding simultaneously.

The process of interpretation obviously involves a subjective element. Even in the selection of the data considered relevant to the event (to say nothing of the prior decision that a particular event is worth investigating) this subjective element comes into play, and it is in operation throughout the process.

As Collingwood says, the historian finds things out by "torturing" the evidence;[34] he subjects all the data

[33]Morris R. Cohen, *op. cit.*, p. 65.
[34]Collingwood, *op. cit.*, pp. 269–70.

to questions suggested to him by what he has learned from the data already examined (in other words, from the facts already established). "Every time the historian asks a question, he asks it because he thinks he can answer it,"[35] writes Collingwood, and illustrates what he means by telling a detective story.[36]

Two quotations, from writers holding different points of view, will serve to underline the necessity of recognizing this subjective element in historiography.[37]

Facts must not only be selected by the researcher but classified, or arranged in certain categories. Otherwise they are meaningless. The trick is, of course, to perform this necessary task of putting facts together without having subordinated historical reality to the caprice of the personality involved.[38]

What is important is not that historiography should be disinterested—which would mean precisely that it would be uninteresting; but that it should be inspired by some really significant and worthy human interest. The historian's aim should not be to have no suppositions, but rather to have the right ones.[39]

The last sentence in each of these quotations draws attention to the fact that the subjective element is not

[35]*ibid.*, p. 281.

[36]*ibid.*, pp. 266–73. The parallel between the historian and the detective is drawn out in detail by Josephine Tey (pseud. for Elizabeth Mackintosh), *The Daughter of Time* (London: Peter Davies Ltd., 1951).

[37]cf. R. M. Hare's discussion of the place which *bliks* have in all cogitation. A. Flew and A. Macintyre (ed.), *New Essays in Philosophical Theology* (London: S.C.M. Press Ltd., 1955), pp. 99–103.

[38]Urban, *op. cit.*, p. 20.

[39]John Baillie, *The Interpretation of Religion* (Edinburgh: T. & T. Clark, 1929), pp. 127–8.

the only one. The historian is not free to make any interpretation, and so arrive at any facts he likes: what he has before him are *data*, not *desiderata*; and he is bound, in so far as he recognizes historiography to be a search for truth, to take care that his interpretation, as well as his inevitable suppositions, are continually checked by the data and not imposed upon them. A historian is therefore called upon to be objective in the sense which that word commonly bears in informed conversation.[40]

Historical enquiry is, as Collingwood says, both empirical and *a priori*.[41] It is empirical because it must rest on the evidence of such things as documents; it is *a priori* because it contains certain assumptions.

The possibility of any fact being used as a datum and so being interpreted in a new way, or even dismissed altogether, has already been referred to. This possibility introduces an element of uncertainty into all historical knowledge.

It may be said that there are some facts concerning which we have an unshakable certainty—a certainty due to what M. C. D'Arcy calls "the infinity of indirect references".[42]

A number of items in our experience are so commonplace and so bound up with all that we think and discover that we seldom advert to them and hardly ever refer to them in our conversa-

---

[40]If however the word is more narrowly defined to imply complete freedom from the mental climate of one's age, objectivity is impossible for the historian. "As this is not what is normally meant by the word objective, the historian need not be disturbed by the sceptic's charge that historical writing cannot be objective." T. A. Roberts, *History and Christian Apologetic*, p. 46.

[41]Collingwood, *op. cit.*, pp. 109–10, 117–18, et. al.

[42]D'Arcy first propounded this in *The Nature of Belief*; he discusses it summarily in *The Sense of History*, pp. 55–7.

tions and relations with others. If, for example, I tell another that I am going to Paris I do not mention all the pieces of knowledge which must hold true if my statement is to have any meaning or be possible. He has not to be told that Paris is the capital of France, that it is a city with houses and human beings living in them, that it takes a certain time to get there, that there are various means of travelling and innumerable other facts which form the web of my simple statement. Our worlds of discourse and connected sense vary, but there are some facts made so obvious by the infinity of indirect references which support them that it is inconceivable to us that they could be untrue. We cannot prove these obvious statements, not for want of evidence but because we have too much.[43]

Similar in texture, D'Arcy adds, are the certainties of space and time.[44] Some things

have been continually presupposed in statements about other places and events and by indirect reference they have grown in certainty with our general growth in knowledge ... We cannot doubt the existence in the past of persons like Napoleon and Queen Victoria. Too many other truths would vanish if their place in history became empty.[45]

Bultmann appears to be similarly confident that there can be certainty in regard to parts of the historical process.

It is possible, for instance, to fix objectively the

---

[43]*ibid.*, p. 55.
[44]D'Arcy also states that these are "of a different order", but it seems to me that the epistemological process is the same.
[45]*ibid.* p. 56.

fact and the time at which Socrates drank the cup of hemlock, the fact and the time when Caesar crossed the Rubicon, the fact and the time when Luther affixed his ninety-five theses to the door of the Castle-Church of Wittenberg, or to know objectively the fact that and the time when a certain battle was fought or a certain empire was founded or a certain catastrophe happened.[46]

He then goes on to say that he does not think that history "is sufficiently seen when it is only seen as a field of such events and actions as can be fixed in space and time."[47]

These statements by D'Arcy and Bultmann so appeal to our commonsense that we may not find it easy to persist in the contention that there is an element of uncertainty about every historical fact. But this is the case—and not only in regard to historical facts. Even our knowledge of objects before us here and now is tinged with a measure of uncertainty: that round tower which I see may turn out on closer examination to be a square one; this piece of gold-bearing rock which I hold in my hand may in fact be only iron pyrites. In every case my knowledge is what I have arrived at by my interpretation of the data; and it is always possible that some new datum, or a more adequate interpretation of the existing data, will lead me to a new fact.

[46]Rudolf Bultmann, *History and Eschatology*, p. 116.
[47]*ibid.* cf. Collingwood's distinction between the "outside" and the "inside" of events (*supra*, pp. 78–9) and Butterfield's contention that, though "technical history and historical research . . . provide us with a reasonable assurance that certain things did happen . . . , for the sum of our ideas and beliefs about the march of ages we need the poet and the prophet, the philosopher and the theologian." *Christianity and History*, p. 23.

What is thus true of a present object is *a fortiori* the case in regard to a past event because (as much of our earlier discussion has made plain) there is so much the greater possibility of new data calling for a fresh interpretation. D'Arcy's "infinity of indirect references" means that so many data are available, and so many facts have been established, that it is inconceivable to us that any new datum could emerge to show them all to be false. And I cannot think that Bultmann means anything else when he speaks of what "strict methodical research can recognize objectively".[48] In practice we have what D'Arcy calls an "unshakable certainty" about these facts; but we must acknowledge that the basis of every fact is what we have established from the data so far available to us. There is always, even in regard to the most "assured" facts, the possibility that new data will show the knowledge we have to need correction.

This possibility—in many cases remote but nevertheless always present—that at some time new data, or renewed consideration of the existing data (in other words, the use as data of currently established facts), may lead to different facts, is what we have in mind when we affirm that in all our knowledge, including our historical knowledge, there is an element of uncertainty.

Uncertainty in the knower is not the same as uncertainty or unreality in the known; and an event is no less real or historical because the historian is uncertain about it. In historical knowledge we have as high a degree of certainty as is possible for the human mind in regard to knowledge of any matter—assuming, of course, that in particular cases we have adequate data at our disposal. Historical knowledge is subject to a

[48] *op. cit.*, p. 116.

lesser degree of certainty than our knowledge of other matters only in that the data presented to us are more often in patent conflict, and can rarely be so easily checked as to their reliability. What we do in the case of conflicting data is to bring other data into the enquiry (if possible) and check our interpretation: thus we establish our facts. This means rejection of some data (which, in a sound interpretation, involves explaining how they emerged in the first place).

In this way, as John McIntyre points out, "the probability factor inherent in the original data will then transfer itself to the total interpretation to which they have given rise. At this level, the problem will be not so much one of probability, as of truth and falsehood"[49]—a problem to be answered, it may be added, by the use of the empirical and *a priori* elements in combination which has already been described.

"The past cannot guarantee its own authenticity," writes Urban. "Only the trained observer armed with present evidence can do that."[50]

The foregoing discussion has made it plain that the relationship between historiography and the historian is a close one—such that any idea of there being an "objective past", which the historian has the duty only to observe and note, must be rejected. It is clear that the historian himself plays an important part in the historiographical process.

Now the historian who plays so large a part can never work with the cold impartiality of an electronic brain which will interpret data in the same way as any other

[49]John McIntyre, "Christ and History", *The Reformed Theological Review*, vol. VIII, no. 3 (August 1949), p. 35.
[50]Urban, *op. cit.*, p. 17.

machine of the same kind (though even an electronic brain has a "memory" such that its answer on any occasion is affected by what it has been called upon to do before—to say nothing of the way the programmer may "pre-set" it to give particular answers). The historian is always a human person, and upon the sort of person he is depends the decision he makes.

One relevant factor is what D'Arcy calls "circum-ambient knowledge". He says of the historical work done on the Bayeux Tapestry:

> The lettering, for instance, in the inscriptions on the tapestry are for the most part square capitals in the Latin tongue. To interpret them requires a knowledge of Latin letters and the meaning of Latin words and sentences. The knowledge of them did not come from some native or God-given intuition; somehow or other men come to have no doubt that a curious shape stands for a letter of the alphabet, and that there is a Latin language with features which are peculiar to the age in which it was written.[51]

There is no need to cite other examples; it is plain that advance in knowledge depends upon knowledge already acquired; and the knowledge any particular historian has affects his ability to give an interpretation of the data before him.

He is moreover from the very start led to approach each datum in a particular way. As we said earlier, immediately any data present themselves for examination they become subject to the process of interpretation. In Bultmann's terms, the historian's "life-relation" (*Lebensverhältnis*) to the matter involves him in a "pre-understanding" (*Vorverständnis*) of it.

[51]M. C. D'Arcy, *op. cit.*, p. 38.

Each interpretation is guided by a certain interest, by a certain *putting of the question*: What is my interest in interpreting the documents? Which question directs me to approach the text? It is evident that the questioning arises from a particular interest in the matter referred to, and therefore that a particular understanding of the matter is presupposed. I like to call this a pre-understanding.[52]

The possession of this sort of knowledge and pre-understanding in no way disqualifies a man from being a historian; indeed, he cannot be a historian without them. True, lack of knowledge and a wrong pre-understanding may lead to wrong conclusions; but this danger is not obviated by fruitless attempts to approach the subject as though one had no knowledge or pre-understanding at all. The safeguard against this danger is, as Cohen says, "to explore one's preconceptions, to make them explicit, to consider their alternatives, and thus to multiply the number of hypotheses available for the apprehension of historical significance."[53] The picture of the past is false, Bultmann says, only when the historian takes his own pre-understanding for a final understanding.[54]

One may not always be conscious of one's preconceptions, one may revise them in the light of the facts which one establishes, and one may be able in some measure to imagine what the facts would be were one possessed of different preconceptions, but one simply cannot undertake the work of a historian

[52]Rudolf Bultmann, *History and Eschatology*, p. 113. See also, *Jesus Christ and Mythology*, p. 50.

[53]Morris R. Cohen, *op. cit.*, p. 80.

[54]R. Bultmann, "Ist voraussetzunglose Exegese möglich?" *Theologische Zeitschrift*, vol. XIII (1957), p. 414.

without being the man that one is—*this* man, with his credulity, his culture, his sophistication, and so on. As Knox has written:

> A poet, or a philosopher, or a saint may in a given case be able to grasp the real meaning of a historical event better than a particular historian. But to the historian who is also poet, or philosopher, or saint, possibilities of understanding are open to which no saint, philosopher, or poet who is not also a historian could conceivably attain.[55]

And if the historian be a man of Christian faith, this fact will inevitably and quite properly play its part in helping him to determine what is significant, what is possible, and what are the facts, about the historical Jesus.

Historiography and the Historical Jesus

The discussion which has occupied us in this chapter was embarked upon because of the assertion that there are parts of the New Testament picture of Jesus which historiographical science cannot accept as true. This assertion implies that, unless these parts (and the uniqueness of Jesus to which they point) can be demonstrated as beyond the criteria of historiography, they must be dismissed as false. There is however another possibility: that of revising the assertion itself, and it is in this direction that our discussion has led. In the light of it we can say the following things about our knowledge of the historical Jesus:

(a) The historical Jesus is an event and, as with all events, there can never be complete knowledge of it. He remains always a challenge to every effort at

[55] John Knox, *Criticism and Faith*, p. 93.

knowing what he was, and historiography must confess that its facts stand in only an analogous relationship to the reality.

(b) As with all events, the historical Jesus is not immediately present to the historian. While the believer may claim an immediacy of relationship with him, this must be always a "mediated immediacy" or a "reflexive immediacy"[1]—an immediacy which has to be understood in terms of a life lived nineteen hundred years ago. And that life, the historical event, can never be put before the historian for his direct scrutiny; it can be known to him only through interpretation of the data which relate to it.

(c) The event of the historical Jesus is, like all events, unique: it occurred but once, and it can never be reproduced. In so far as it can be compared with anything, it can only be along the line of the continuum of human analogy—notably most various and unpredictable.

(d) If it is concluded that some things said of this event could not possibly have taken place, this is a judgment by the individual historian. This historian may have his judgment supported by the judgments of other historians as well as by reasons drawn from what he knows generally; but it is open to another historian, who also has his reasons, to declare that such and such a thing could have happened. Both historians must be prepared to state and defend the grounds upon which their judgments concerning possibility rest, but no man can determine the judgment to be made by any other.

(e) Whatever conclusion is drawn concerning the significance of the historical Jesus is also a judgment by an individual historian, and while he must be

[1]See *infra*, pp. 137-40.

prepared to state and defend the grounds upon which his judgment rests, no one else can determine his judgment for him. The Christian historian has as much right as any other to enter a judgment on this matter, and to claim (probably meaning by this that the living of this life has consequences which affect or should affect all people) that the historical Jesus lived a life of greater significance than anyone else.

(f) The facts at which the Christian arrives concerning the historical Jesus are no less facts than those at which the non-Christian arrives. In each case the fact is established by interpretation of data, so that differences are to be discussed in terms of the data considered and the adequacy of the interpretation. It is not sufficient to dismiss certain facts as impossible of acceptance by any historian.

(g) Whatever facts are established by the historian are contemporary with himself so that his picture of the historical Jesus, though a reconstruction of an event that is past, is itself an event of the present. It may be added that this present event is part of the response to the past event; and together they constitute an event which is not yet finished.

All this should incline us to treat a good deal more cautiously than some have done the contention that it is impossible for the divinity of Jesus to be disclosed along with the humanity, or for what is sometimes called the superhistorical to be one with the historical. We may fairly conclude that those who have run to the concept of "super-history" have moved there too speedily: we do not need to postulate a type of history free from the ordinary criteria of historiography in order to retain the Christian conviction that faith has a historical basis.

III

Immediacy and Faith

OUR CRITIQUE OF HISTORIOGRAPHY has shown
that there can be made out a better case than some
have conceded for asserting that knowledge of what
was unique about Jesus is as soundly based as knowledge
of anything else about him.

But it has also shown that much the same thing
(that he was both like and unlike other men) is to be
said concerning any other historical figure. Of any
other figure it must be said also that, though
the events are past, the situation in which the facts
are established is a present one; there is therefore a
sense in which every figure of the past becomes a
contemporary of the historian who learns about him.

If it be now asked whether the historical Jesus
contemporary to the Christian historian is present to
him in any way different from that in which, say,
Julius Caesar is present to the historian interested
in the conquests of Rome, the answer is that he is
present in the same way and yet in a different way.

He is present in the same way because the same
epistemological processes and historiographical criteria
determine what facts are to be established concerning
him.

He is present in a different way because of that

uniqueness to which we have referred—a uniqueness which must affect peculiarly every relationship to him. Since this uniqueness is evidently different from the sort of uniqueness which attaches to *every* historical event, we must show more clearly just what is meant by it.

In the following pages we shall clarify the concept of "uniqueness" as it is applied to Jesus by drawing upon some other terms used of him, and shall introduce as the definitive concept that of "immediacy". We shall then show how this immediacy is recognized, and the nature of the factor bringing about the recognition. The last section of this chapter will introduce some relevant points concerning the Christian Church.

Uniqueness and Immediacy

Our first task is to consider what we mean when as Christians we refer to the uniqueness of Jesus.

We must make it plain that we do not wish to attribute to Jesus such a uniqueness as marks him off absolutely from other men.

A tendency to do this is discernible at many points in Christian history. Docetism, against which there are protests within the New Testament itself,[1] is one expression of it. It is seen again in Modalism, in Apollinarianism, and in Eutycheanism, all of which the Church wisely rejected. We may discern the same tendency at work in the Reformed insistence upon the *non posse peccare*,[2] and in the manner of argument

---

[1] I John 1.1; 4.2,3; II John 7.
[2] This was set against the idea of *posse non peccare*, and held to because it was felt that if Christ could sin, and so fail in the office of Mediator, the foundations of salvation could be overturned.

whereby some of our contemporaries support belief in the miracles and the Virgin Birth of Jesus—if indeed such a manner of argument is not to be discerned at some points in the New Testament itself.

Such a tendency is deserving of our sympathy and its motive of our commendation: every Christian wants to cry with Noetus: "What evil do I do when I glorify Christ?" There is a uniqueness about Jesus; and some quick to condemn the forms in which this tendency has expressed itself have been in danger of obscuring something integral to a Christian's understanding of Jesus.

Nonetheless, it is with the opponents, and not with the protagonists, of this tendency that we take our stand—and that also because of something integral to a Christian's understanding of Jesus. Whatever uniqueness attaches to Jesus he is "consubstantial with us concerning the manhood"; without this the idea of the Word becoming flesh is an illusory one.

What we do mean by the uniqueness of Jesus will be disclosed as we consider some of the terms which have been used concerning him.

We could start with the terms used in the New Testament and go on to draw out the meaning implied in each. But this would not advance materially our present purpose, which is to show how this uniqueness bears upon historical knowledge of Jesus rather than to uncover all that may be involved in the use of any particular term. And in any case there are available the results of labours of others in this field.[3] What

[3]See especially: Vincent Taylor, *The Names of Jesus* (London: Macmillan & Co. Ltd., 1953); Oscar Cullman, *The Christology of the New Testament*, trans. S. C. Guthrie and C. A. M. Hall (London: S.C.M. Press Ltd., 1959).

Taylor says concerning "the principal names and titles of Jesus" can be said concerning them all:

A man, revered, loved and worshipped, is described by a terminology which bends and cracks under the strain, because it is being used to describe a unique person, and therefore to serve an end for which, humanly speaking, it was not intended from the standpoint of its history.[4]

Or we could take other terms which have been used at various times in reference to Jesus and draw out what each has to contribute to our understanding of his uniqueness. The developed usages of practically all the biblical terms, the θεάνθρωπος of Origen, the "two natures, one person" of Chalcedon, the *multivolipraesentia* of Chemnitz, the *Urbild* of Schleiermacher, the *Führer* of Heim—each one of these, and the many others which have been used, may have something to contribute to our understanding of Jesus' uniqueness; and the fact that so many different ideas have been called forth suggests that none has proved wholly adequate.

It is however doubtful whether the adding of term upon term would bring us appreciably nearer our goal. Actually, almost any one of them can be regarded as the primary one, and the others used to explain the peculiar connotation it must be given when applied to Jesus; the development of Christology (particularly that section of it called the Person of Christ) has been largely the bringing in of new terms to clear away misunderstandings grown up about older ones. What we shall do is look at two ideas which are particularly useful for understanding what place Jesus has in

[4]Taylor, *ibid.*, p. 70.

history. These two are the ideas of "fulfilment" and of "centrality".

The idea of fulfilment, as applied to Jesus, is a very old one belonging, McIntyre says, "to the very givenness of the situation in which Christ was first known by men for what he really was"; it is moreover "the ultimate basis upon which rest all the other Christological affirmations that we make."[5]

Certainly the idea of Jesus as fulfilling the law and the prophets had a prominent place in the New Testament and was used a great deal by the first generation of Christian preachers as well as by many of later generations. But since the nineteenth century (when the Old Testament writers came to be studied more for what they thought themselves to be saying than for the cryptic references they made to future events) it has suffered something of a decline. Yet the idea of fulfilment (in somewhat different senses[6]) has not been without its exponents in contemporary writing, and there is no doubt that it is an idea which sheds light upon the place of Jesus in history.

To provide a starting-point for our own discussion of this concept we shall note what Emil Brunner has to say in a chapter entitled "Revelation as Fulfilment: Jesus Christ".[7]

[5] John McIntyre, *The Christian Doctrine of History*, p. 49. Cf. H. P. Owen: "Almost all the Christological titles of the New Testament imply a belief in Christ as the Fulfiller. The offence and truth of Christ's Person are one with the offence and truth of fulfilment. It is no accident that Marcion was a Docetist." *Revelation and Existence*, p. 125.
[6] See, for example, McIntyre's discussion of the views of John Marsh, A. G. Hebert, H. R. Mackintosh and Rudolf Bultmann; *op. cit.*, pp. 45-76.
[7] Emil Brunner, *Revelation and Reason*, trans. Olive Wyon (London: S.C.M. Press Ltd., 1947), chapter VIII, pp. 95-118.

Brunner begins by noting how insistent the New Testament is upon the declaration that God has finally and completely revealed himself in the person of Jesus. The relationship of this revelation to general revelation (or the revelation in creation) is one of identity as far as the Revealer is concerned, but of difference in the form of the revelation: by comparison the general revelation is impersonal, non-historical and static, and it provides no answer to the question of what God intends to do with us sinful human beings. The relationship between the revelation in Jesus and that in the Old Testament is one neither of identity nor of contradiction; it is expressed in the category of promise and fulfilment: "That which has been fulfilled is the same as that which had been foretold, it is true, because it was the goal of prophecy; but at the same time it is something entirely different, because it is a present reality, and no longer merely a vision of the future." It is inadequate to think of the revelation in Jesus as consisting in the fact that he was the greatest teacher of mankind, or the perfect example, neither of which categories rises above human possibilities; the biblical idea of the prophet is the disclosure of a mystery from the world beyond, and Jesus is more than a prophet.[8] While the prophet disappears behind his message, in Jesus message and

[8] *ibid.*, p. 101. In a footnote Brunner says that the primitive Church described this categorical uniqueness of Jesus by the title of "Christ-Messiah, Son of God and Lord", and that the fact of his self-consciousness on this point is not affected by the question whether he actually used these titles of himself. (It is strange that Brunner uses the phrase "more than a prophet" peculiarly of Jesus (and goes on to say on p. 102 that "to be '*more* than a prophet' . . . can only mean that the person who speaks and the content of his message are *one*") when the New Testament uses this phrase only of John Baptist.)

person are one: "He himself comes forth from the mystery of transcendence, just as previously the prophetic word had issued thence." Real authority is impossible within the purely human sphere, and resides only in the prophetic word, which can reach a higher degree of authority only when the authority of the word is transferred to the person who utters it and in the person of Jesus the person of God himself encounters us.

As the fulfiller of the promises of the Old Testament revelation, Christ is made known to us in his threefold office: he is the messianic king, who rules in self-giving generous love; he is the end of the Israelite priesthood and sacrificial system; he is the prophet who is the real bearer of the revelation. The four elements in the Old Testament revelation which seem to point beyond themselves to a hidden and as yet unrealized unity (the word, the act, the name and the face) have become a unity in Jesus, and in so doing for the first time have received their full meaning. If God reveals himself in Jesus and not merely through him, then in him we encounter God in person, and he himself is God: thus the doctrine of the person of Jesus as God-man is the New Testament concept of revelation made explicit in Christology.

Brunner concludes his chapter by showing that it is not until we reach the New Testament that the subjective side of revelation is clearly recognized and gathered up in a comprehensive idea.

Using the presentation of Brunner as a basis, we may note the following as the significant ideas in the concept of fulfilment.

(a) Jesus is the fulfilment of human knowledge concerning God. What is made known in him is at one with what may be known of God from other sources.

Brunner's use of the terms "general revelation" and "revelation in creation" may seem to plunge us into the continuing debate (especially as it has taken form between himself and Karl Barth) concerning the place of "natural theology". But it will not serve our purpose to follow that debate here for what is in dispute does not affect the point which is important: that involved in the idea of fulfilment is the assertion that the new thing Jesus makes known is not something foreign to the nature of God.

(b) Jesus is the fulfilment of all disclosures of mystery from the world beyond.

Any knowledge of the divine must come to us from beyond the sphere which is at the disposal of man; this leads Brunner to say that within this sphere there is no real authority, for what is there called by that name simply refers to the fact that there are individuals who at present know more than other people (and who may be outstripped by others tomorrow). Thus it is the prophetic word alone which has absolute authority, and Jesus' fulfilment of the prophetic word rests in his having the only possible "higher degree of authority": the unity of him who speaks and the word that is spoken.

While the nature of Brunner's discussion at that point leads him to consider only the prophets of the Old Testament, what he has to say concerning Jesus as the fulfilment of their words can be applied to any disclosure of truth about God. Thus, if we agree with Clement of Alexandria that "philosophy was a 'schoolmaster' to bring the Greek mind to Christ as the Law brought the Hebrews,"[9] we shall say that Jesus was

[9] *Stromateis* i. 28.

the fulfilment of Greek philosophy, in that what was there said truly about God was given more perfect expression in the deeds and sayings of Jesus. There are indications that such a general category of fulfilment was present to the minds of some New Testament writers,[10] and it is one which makes the concept of fulfilment more acceptable to many Christians. It may be added, in respect both of the Old Testament and of any other "prophetic words", that it is because we see in Jesus the fulfilment of them that we recognize them to have been true and endued with that authority which we appreciate as "real" or "absolute".[11]

It is in the recognition of Jesus as the fulfilment of disclosures from the world beyond that there lies the basis for assertions concerning his person. For this fulfilment—the idea of Jesus as "more than a prophet"—means that the person having this "higher degree of authority" is one with God.

(c) Specifically, Jesus is the fulfilment of what was promised in the Old Testament.

Whatever may be thought of the more general category of fulfilment, the emphasis upon this specific category in the New Testament is apparent to all, and its prominence there has led to its wide acceptance by Christians and its use by them in their proclamation of the Gospel. For some, it is the only meaning that fulfilment has.

The factors Brunner uses in exposition of this aspect of fulfilment are the "three-fold office", and the four elements of the word, the act, the name and

[10] John 1.9,10; Romans 1.21, 22; Ephesians 3.9,10.

[11] To say that it is because of their fulfilment in Jesus that *we* recognize them as authoritative is not to deny that, by others without the Christian revelation, they may have been recognized as authoritative on some other grounds.

the face. Strands of Old Testament thought which have been used by other writers to the same end include the account of the Exodus, the description of the Suffering Servant, the Messianic promises, the covenant and the kingdom of God. In regard to each it has been held that whatever significance it had before the coming of Jesus, it is now seen to have been endowed with richer significance. The use of such categories by modern writers points to the departure from the old conception of "fulfilment", wherein a number of particular statements were cited (with various degrees of ingenuity) to prove prophetic prediction of details in the life of Jesus.

(d) There is also involved in the idea of fulfilment that of more than fulfilment. While Jesus is recognized as the perfection of all that had gone before, he is recognized also as going beyond what had been anticipated.

This is implicit in what has already been said but it deserves to be mentioned separately, if for no other reason than to avoid any suggestion that all that Jesus was could have been foreseen. This would be as false to any Christian concept of fulfilment as the suggestion that Jesus was the inevitable outcome of some process which was at work before his coming.

It is this fact of fulfilment being more than fulfilment to which Bultmann draws attention when he speaks of prophecy being fulfilled in "its inner contradiction, its miscarriage",[12] and to which McIntyre refers more accurately (since it can hardly be said of the prophecy itself that it is contradictory; it is the manner of its

---

[12]Rudolf Bultmann, "Prophecy and Fulfilment", *Essays Philosophical and Theological* (London: S.C.M. Press Ltd., 1955), p. 205.

fulfilment which introduces this idea[13]) when he speaks of the "polarity of fulfilment".

According to this notion, fulfilment has two poles, positive and negative, so that fulfilment stands in this double relation to prophecy of both affirming it and denying it. What in fact happens is that fulfilment affirms certain aspects of the prophetic message and denies other parts, but the affirmation and the negation are so interwoven that it is impossible to establish any point-to-point correlation between the confirmation and what is confirmed, or between the negation and what is negated. It is therefore impossible to save the confirmation and throw away the negation; both are necessary parts in the polarity of fulfilment.[14]

The second of the two ideas we have selected as particularly useful for our purpose is that of centrality.

Nels Ferré has developed this concept in his book *Christ and the Christian*,[15] where he speaks repeatedly of Jesus as "the centre of history".[16] Two quotations will put his position before us succinctly:

He is the exceptional Event that transformingly fulfils, clarifies and transforms the past and, as history's centre, offers a full Gospel for all mankind.[17]

The eternal purpose which God purposed before the creation of the world is thus fulfilled

---

[13]As Bultmann himself remarks on p. 206.

[14]John McIntyre, *The Christian Doctrine of History*, pp. 70–1.

[15]Nels F. S. Ferré, *Christ and the Christian* (London: Collins, 1958).

[16]e.g., pp. 167, 172, 199, 201, 208, 235. Other terms used by Ferré are "the Event-Meaning" (p. 24) and "the Consummation" (p. 241).

[17]*op. cit.*, p. 199.

in Jesus as the Christ, the centre of history, the usherer in of a new and final stage.[18]

As these words show, the ideas of fulfilment and centrality are not far apart; thought of a "centre of history" is bound to involve the idea of its being in close relationship with what has gone before.

It may be asked therefore how the idea of centrality adds to understanding of Jesus' uniqueness. It does so in at least three ways.[19]

"Centrality" suggests more clearly than "fulfilment" that Jesus' place in history is not only that of the one in whom the prophecies of the Old Testament have been realized. It is true, as we have seen, that the idea of fulfilment may refer to all disclosures of truth about God but it is the prophetic word of the Old Testament that is most in mind when that term is used. Centrality, on the other hand, suggests that Jesus' relationship to the course of history is seen in a much wider context.

Again, the use of the term "centre" points more obviously to what is the determinative factor—namely, Jesus himself.

The idea of fulfilment (particularly when the matter of "polarity of fulfilment" is kept in mind) does allow us to assert that his coming was a divine intrusion. Nonetheless some presentations of him as fulfilment (following a line suggested by the ἵνα πληρωθῇ[20] of the Scriptures) give the impression that the predic-

---

[18]op. cit., pp. 200-1.
[19]In line with our earlier suggestion (supra, p. 124) that almost any term used of Jesus can be regarded as the primary one and the others used to explain it, we could regard what is said under the heading of centrality as designed to clear away misunderstandings which have grown up concerning the concept of fulfilment.
[20]Matthew 1.22; Mark 14.49; Luke 24.44; John 12.38; et al.

tions were the really determinative factor, Jesus himself being but the end-term in a process which, having
started, moves on inexorably to its conclusion; "fulfilment" does not suggest plainly that what has gone
before is to be understood in the light of what takes
place at the centre.

The idea of centrality has the third advantage of
indicating clearly that Jesus is the determinative factor
in regard to what takes place after his coming.[21]
History, says Preiss, is a drama having "a centre which
is also its origin and its ending."[22]

As Ferré puts it:

The coming of Christ the Centre nevertheless
does not mean that history is done because the
fulness has come. The coming of the Centre
entails rather the absolute command to proceed
at the fastest possible rate toward that centre.
History does not become still, but only more
mobile, when the fixed point of God's final
purpose is staked at its potential centre once for
all.[23]

And Paul: it is God's "loving design, centred in
Christ, to give history its fulfilment by resuming
everything in him, all that is in heaven, all that is on
earth, summed up in him."[24]

The ideas we have considered help us to see what
Christians have in mind when they speak of Jesus'

[21]Oscar Cullmann's picture of this centre as the decisive battle in
a war which must continue until "Victory Day" has become a
common way of expressing this truth. *Christ and Time*, p. 84.
[22]Th. Preiss, "The Vision of History in the New Testament", *On
the Meaning of History*, ed. H. Kraemer (Geneva: Oikumene,
1949), p. 54.
[23]Nels F. S. Ferré, *op. cit.*, pp. 235-6.
[24]Ephesians 1.9,10, as rendered by D'Arcy, *op. cit.*, p. 270.

uniqueness. One way of summing this up is to say that his place in the historical process is to make known to all men the truth about their own place in it.

Amplification of this last phrase would deflect from our present purpose, since it would extend to every facet of what the Christian thinks about God, man and the universe. It will be sufficient here to remark that the truth about any man's place in the historical process includes convictions concerning his responsibility towards the Creator, his failure to measure up to that responsibility, the Creator's readiness to forgive and renew him as he acknowledges his failure, and the goodness and mercy that follow him all his days. Jesus' place is to make men aware of such things, and to be aware of them is to apprehend the uniqueness of Jesus.

Clearly, any historian who establishes this fact concerning Jesus is himself involved in a particular relationship to him, and we shall presently consider in some detail what this is.[25] Meanwhile let us observe that the uniqueness of Jesus may be looked at from two points of view.

One point of view is to say that Jesus is unique because of his unique relationship to God. This line of thinking would lead to development of a doctrine of the Person but, attractive as that has shown itself to theologians of many generations, it is not the line that we shall follow.

We are bound to say, however, that it is this aspect of Jesus' uniqueness which is the determinative one. "Fulfilment", "centrality", and whatever other concepts are applied to Jesus, including particularly the classical concept of "divinity", all point to him as

[25]*infra*, p. 137-40.

one whose being as a man in history is due to the peculiar intervention of God.

The "divinity" was not half his nature or a second nature, but was that purpose and activity of God which made the event which happened around him, but also in him and through him, the saving event it was. The divinity of Jesus was the deed of God. The uniqueness of Jesus was the absolute uniqueness of what God did in him.[26]

A distinction between the "Person" and the "Work" of Jesus cannot be strictly maintained; nevertheless Brunner is right in saying that the way which the knowledge of Jesus has actually taken in the past, and the right way, leads from the Work to the Person.[27]

But here, as is often the case, the *ordo cognoscendi* is not the same as the *ordo essendi*. What Jesus did was because of what he was, and the uniqueness of his relationship to the historian is dependent upon the uniqueness of Jesus' own relationship to God. That is what we mean when we say that this aspect of his uniqueness is the determinative one.

It has already been stated however that the development of this aspect is not the line we shall follow here. There are two reasons for this.

For one thing, there seems to be something unnecessarily presumptuous about any attempt to express just what may be involved in Jesus' relationship to God. When H. R. Mackintosh and P. T. Forsyth[28]

[26]John Knox, *The Death of Christ*, p. 123.
[27]Emil Brunner, *Die Christliche Lehre von Schöpfung und Erlösung* (Zürich: Zwingli-Verlag, 1950), pp. 317–18. *The Christian Doctrine of Creation and Redemption*, trans. Olive Wyon (London: Lutterworth Press, 1952), pp. 271–2.
[28]H. R. Mackintosh, *The Doctrine of the Person of Jesus Christ* (Edinburgh: T. & T. Clark, 1913), p. 466.

criticized some of their predecessors in the Kenotic line of Christology for their efforts to body forth just what the Son of God must have undergone in becoming man, they expressed what we readily recognize as a proper attitude. Many a heresy—and a cold orthodoxy —have arisen because it was thought that something definite and precise could be said about this.

But our chief reason for not pursuing this line further is that questions of this kind do not bear directly upon our present study. Our concern here is to trace the uniqueness of the relationship in which Jesus stands to the historian, and we shall do that more effectively if we restrict ourselves to considering Jesus as he is in the present situation; we shall therefore as far as possible pass over consideration of how he may have attained that stature, as well as of what has been called the Achilles' heel of any Christology: the question of what consciousness Jesus may have had of his uniqueness.

I have said that this restriction of our interest will be "as far as possible"; this qualification is necessary because of the great difficulty there is in keeping these two things separate—as indeed the terms of our own presentation have already shown.

Although the point of view we have just considered is the determinative aspect of Jesus' uniqueness, it is not the only one.

It is possible also to consider his uniqueness from the point of view of his relationship to us and to the history of which we are part. While (as we have suggested) any term rightly used of Jesus will point to the fact of a divine intervention in him, almost every term originates in its descriptive relevance to Jesus as we see him; the terms "fulfilment" and "centrality" are clear examples of this.

To characterize this aspect of Jesus' uniqueness (his relationship to the believing historian) the term "immediacy" is the one most appropriate to a situation which is, in Knox's terms, event-plus-response, and, in our own terms, fact-established-by-interpretation-of-data.

Examination of this immediacy shows that there is involved in it the kind of immediacy demanded of all objects of religious belief. As Norman MacLeish has pointed out, any judgments concerning God are believed to be judgments concerning an external reality;[29] no religious person ever concludes that what he thinks about God is only a result of wishful thinking. Religion cannot exist in the absence of a conviction that there is here at hand something (or somebody) towards which adoration and trust (or fear) can be directed.

Jesus has, for the Christian believer, this kind of immediacy.

But the immediacy in which Jesus stands to the believer also involves another factor: one which we may refer to, in a phrase used by John Baillie, as "mediated immediacy".[30]

To appreciate this we shall pause briefly to consider the place of media in our coming to knowledge of God.[31]

When the glory of a sunset leads me to bow in adoration of the God who has created such things I

---

[29]Norman MacLeish, *The Nature of Religious Knowledge* (Edinburgh: T. & T. Clark, 1938), p. 4.

[30]John Baillie, *Our Knowledge of God* (London: Oxford University Press, 1939), p. 178.

[31]The next three paragraphs largely reproduce portions of my article, "The Redemptive Mission of the Church", *Scottish Journal of Theology*, vol. x (1957), pp. 156-7.

am convinced that the God whom I thus adore has himself put this evidence of his majesty before me; yet I am covinced also that my adoration arose out of my observing the sunset. Similarly when a particular sermon "strikes home" at this or that aspect of my life, impelling me to the forsaking of some habit or to the taking up of some new responsibility, I am convinced that it is God himself who has spoken to me; yet I am convinced also that the challenge I feel it impossible to disregard came to me only as I listened to that particular sermon.

While examples of this kind could be multiplied, enough has been said to indicate that while the knowledge we have of God is ours because he confronts us with himself, we always have that knowledge given to us as we come by knowledge of other things. Our knowledge of God, then, is both immediate and mediate.

It is *along with*[32] the story of Abraham, or of Daniel, or of some extra-biblical character, that we sense a significance which it has for us here and now; it is *along with* the reading of a passage which Paul or someone else wrote to the Galatians or to Timothy, that we read a message which applies to ourselves; it is *along with* the glory of the sunset that we sense the majesty of creative power, and so on. These are media with which God brings himself to us. They are not, on the one hand, things by means of which we could, unaided, rise to knowledge of God for, unless God himself should decide to use them, they would not be media at all but simply others among the many things which fill our lives. Nor, on the other

---

[32]John Baillie makes use "without prejudice" of the Lutheran phrase, "in, with and under"; *op. cit.*, pp. 178 ff.

hand, are we able to dispense with them, along the mystics' line, as obstacles which hold God away from us. As the media of his choice they play an essential part in the mediating to us of his immediacy, and we have no knowledge of God apart from our knowledge of them.

We do not need to conclude that the event of Jesus is a medium in exactly the same sense as a sunset or the Bible in order to see, from what is said in these paragraphs, that in our relationship to that event there are involved both immediacy and mediacy. There is immediacy because of the relationship to us (a unique one, as we saw) in which he stands as an object of religious trust; and there is mediacy because he, the event, is known by means of the picture of him established by the historian.

It is this which in A. D. Foster's opinion constitutes "the peculiar nature and difficulty of Christianity as an 'historical' religion". By this we mean, he says,

a spirituality which reflects its immediate basis backwards into the past. Thus while all religion is religion of immediacy, historical religion involves reflexive immediacy[33] . . . Immediacy taken alone cannot involve any litigation with a science of the past. Therefore the problem we wish to explore lies, not in faith's direct relation to the portrait of Christ, but in the reflexiveness of faith by which the portrait is projected two millennia backwards in time.[34]

[33]Foster says in a footnote that this seems a more adequate phrase than Baillie's "mediated immediacy", "for the basis of Christianity is mediated in any case, but that might remain a matter of indifference, were it not for the reflexive affirmations of faith concerning the foundation from which the mediation commences."
[34]A. D. Foster, op. cit., pp. 101–2.

Our own discussion of the relationship between Jesus and the believing historian, added to what was earlier disclosed concerning the nature of historical knowledge, leads us to concur in Foster's judgment about "the peculiar nature and difficulty of Christianity". The Christian sees Jesus as unique but remains unshaken in his confidence that he knows this unique person through the normal processes of historiography. For our definitive characterization of this situation we have chosen the concept of mediated immediacy.

Recognition of the Immediacy

We have not yet faced directly the question arising from the fact that not all who consider the historical Jesus arrive at the facts which the Christian does. What are we to say concerning such people? That they fail to see where their thinking should lead them? That, deliberately or unconsciously, they allow some ulterior motive (such as unwillingness to face up to the demands of the Christian ethic) to distort their thinking? No doubt some historians' work is deficient in these respects but the Christian cannot condemn as stupid or dishonest, or both, all who do not concur in his interpretation of the data.

There is another explanation; we shall come to it by discussing briefly the nature of revelation.

In an illuminating article, John McIntyre offers an analysis of the revelational situation in the following terms:[1]

[1]John McIntyre, "Christology and Revelation", *The Reformed Theological Review*, vol. xv (1956), pp. 81–9; vol. xvi (1957), pp. 11–20, 44–52.

It may seem at first sight that the pattern of revelation disclosed in the Old Testament is of this kind: A reveals B to C, where A is the revealer (for example, the drying up of the Red Sea), B is the revealed (God) and C is the recipient of revelation. On further thought, however, we recognize that modification of the formula is required in each of its terms. For it is not A, as A, which reveals God, but A seen in a particular way; thus the first modification must be to change A into xA, "where x denotes the supernatural interpretation of A; if you like, the perpendicular reference which is ignored by the naturalistic thinker." Again, it is not the whole of God's essence (it is to be remembered that McIntyre is at this stage offering an analysis on the basis of the Old Testament) that is revealed in any particular situation, and so our second modification is to change B into yB, "where y symbolizes one aspect of God's nature, one fiat of his will." Thirdly, since "there is from time to time the suggestion made in the Old Testament that C's recognition of xA as revealing yB is not entirely due to C's unaided effort, but to the working of God within C in some directly immanent way," so that his apprehension "is due to a paradoxical combination of intense personal activity and divine spiritual indwelling," it may be as well to modify C to C/IG, where IG symbolizes God's indwelling grace.[2]

Turning to the New Testament McIntyre contends that the formula adduced from the statements of the Old Testament is not adequate, and suggests that we must now have two formulae "to cover the full

[2]This paragraph contains all that McIntyre offers in description of the tantalizing concept represented by "indwelling grace"; it is however sufficient for the purpose of this analysis.

implications of the revelation of God to the believer in Jesus Christ."[3] The first formula is: xA reveals AB to C, where (since A "would represent the human life of Jesus Christ as it is open for inspection by the non-Christian historian and philosopher") the presence of x indicates that that life is regarded as bearing a supra-human significance, and where AB "signifies that in the revelation of God in Jesus Christ God reveals *himself*, not under one or other specific attributes but himself under the limitations, or within the possibilities, of human nature, or rather *a* human nature." But since this formula might include revelations of God which are given through noble personalities other than Jesus, a second formula is needed: AB reveals EB to C, which covers C's assurance that in having to do with Christ he has to do with God himself (that is, in knowing AB he also knows EB, where E is God's essential nature).

There is no need here to discuss McIntyre's presentation in detail, or to indicate the measure of our agreement with its every point. The foregoing summary of it has been included because it illumines certain points to be made in answering the question how recognition of the immediacy of Jesus to the believer is arrived at.

This question arose from our noticing that not all who investigate the events relating to the historical Jesus arrive at the same facts: they do not all become Christians. What is also to be noticed is that those who become Christians do not all consider that their belief is independent of what may be ascertained by investigating those events: they are for the most part of the firm opinion that the uniqueness they see

[3]*ibid.*, vol. XVI, pp. 14-5.

in Jesus is as much historical fact as anything else.

The difference between these two groups, in terms of McIntyre's symbolism, is that one group builds its interpretation on the basis of the data belonging to A, while the other builds on the data belonging to xA. Both have a concern for the data, and both endeavour, by adequate interpretation of them, to reach the proper facts.[4] The difference lies in x, "the unknown factor". We must now see what this factor is.

In Collingwood's analysis of the historiographical process, which is very similar to that which we have developed as our own,[5] he makes the statement that one new fact added to a mass of old ones involves the complete transformation of the old.[6] To this we shall add three comments.

(a) To say that the addition of one new fact involves the complete transformation of the old ones does not mean that these are now seen to have been altogether false. They may well remain as facts which have been rightly established though seen now in a new context and from a different perspective.

(b) Nor does this transformation mean that the old

---

[4]In his book, *The Christian Doctrine of History*, McIntyre refers to this situation in terms of the different "structures" which may be made up by various combinations of the different "categories" (necessity, providence, etc.) which make up historical occurrence. He says: "The inability of the non-Christian to accept the Christian interpretation is not simply due to his love for the lie instead of the truth, but rather to the fact that he really thinks he has the truth himself. Each of the structures is therefore a selection from a complex whole, and selection is made by ignoring the categories which form the other structures." p. 108.

[5]See especially, *supra*, pp. 105-14.

[6]R. G. Collingwood, *The Idea of History*, p. 147. This particular way of putting it occurs as part of his criticism of J. B. Bury whose attempt to bring Gibbon up to date by means of footnotes, Collingwood says, had a result rather like that of adding a saxophone obbligato to an Elizabethan madrigal.

facts are now to be regarded as irrelevant. They may be seen to have a new relevance; and probably the new fact will be meaningless unless considered in relationship to the old ones.

(c) The establishment of a new fact is usually due to the emergence of some new datum or data, though sometimes a new fact arises as the result of a more thorough interpretation of the data which were to hand all the time.

What we have in the case of recognition of the immediacy of Jesus (which is the situation we are discussing) is the transformation of A by x, which, as a new fact, leads the historian to see in a new way all that had been previously established. Thus, for example, the established fact[7] that a birth took place in Bethlehem of Judæa becomes, with the entrance into the situation of x, the fact that the Word became flesh and dwelt among us. And if we recall the comments which we added to Collingwood's statement, we shall recognize: (a) that this transformation does not alter the truth of the fact that a birth took place; (b) that this fact of a birth taking place continues to be relevant to the situation; and (c) that the one fact, like the other, has been arrived at by interpretation of data.

Thus the Christian, seeing the historical Jesus as the unique revelation of God, does not arrive at this understanding by a path which neglects what may be known of Jesus by way of historiography.

Some words of J. M. Robinson call attention to a parallel between the understanding of the historio-

---

[7] That some historians doubt whether Jesus really was born in Bethlehem does not affect the point being made here; we could say generally "the established fact that a man named Jesus lived nineteen hundred years ago."

graphical process we have reached and the preaching of the early Church.

He points out (with particular reference to what he speaks of as "a new quest of the historical Jesus", though what he has to say here is relevant to all attempts to investigate the past) that while modern historiography emphasizes the need to grasp the self-actualization of the participants in the events which it investigates, this does not mean the discontinuing of "objective philological, comparative-religious, and social-historical research".[8]

Contemporary methodology has not discontinued these methods in its new understanding of history, but has merely shifted them more decidedly from ends to means. It is true that the "explanation" of an event or view-point does not consist merely in showing its external causes or identifying the source from which an idea was borrowed. Much of what was once lauded as the "truth" or "reality" of history is now mocked by insight into the genetic fallacy. Yet despite all this, knowledge of the external cause of the detection of the source idea is often indispensable for understanding what was involved at the deeper level. Contemporary methodology consists precisely in the combination and interaction of objective analysis and existential openness, i.e., it seeks historical understanding

[8]The sort of historiography Robinson has in mind may be seen from the following sentences, which occur in an earlier part of his book. "Today history is increasingly understood as essentially the unique and creative, . . . whose truth could not be known by Platonic recollection or inference from a rational principle, but only through historical encounter. History is the act of intention, the commitment, the meaning for the participants, behind the external occurrence." *A New Quest of the Historical Jesus*, p. 67.

precisely in the simultaneous interaction of phenomenological objectivity and existential "objectivity".[9]

It is this sort of "combination and interaction" which takes place when the Christian historian sees the facts of the life of Jesus to be facts having immediate relevance to his own living. He does not disregard what the legitimate pursuit of historiography has to tell him about them, but appreciates this in the context of what the fulness of his own experience has to teach.

In this "interaction of 'Jesus in the context of dead-and-gone first-century Judaism' and 'Jesus as a possible understanding of my existence'," Robinson says, there may be recognized "a formal analogy in terms of modern historiography to the Kerygma's identification of the Jesus of history with the heavenly Lord."[10]

The question which was posed at the beginning of this section can now be answered by saying that what makes the difference between those who recognize the uniqueness, or immediacy, of Jesus and those who do not is the establishment of a new fact, the x in xA, and by adding that this new fact is discerned by what Christians generally call "faith".

In the next two sections we shall consider what faith is and how it arises. But before embarking upon this discussion two things must be noted briefly.

---

[9]*ibid.*, p. 96. In a footnote Robinson remarks that "objectivity resides in a complete openness to what the creative historical event has to say . . . Thus one's historical involvement, not one's disinterestedness, is the instrument leading to objectivity, and it must be constantly observed that this 'subjective participation' of the historian consists precisely in the potential suspension of his own personal views, for the sake of hearing what the other has to tell him about his existence."

[10]*ibid.*, p. 97.

The testimony of those who have seen historical occurrence with the eye of faith is that such a man, in Barth's words, "must regard himself as someone else whom he had no capacity to become,"[11] and hence the capacity to discern this new fact has been designated a gift of God.[12] It is only c/IG[13] who can see $x\text{A}$ as revealing AB.

Our presentation of the manner in which the immediacy of Jesus is recognized could give the impression that every Christian *first* establishes the facts as if he were not a Christian, and *then* adds another fact which transforms them all. This is not always— indeed, it is very rarely—the case. To this, and the question whether there is some minimum knowledge of the A variety without which $x\text{A}$ cannot occur, we shall return; but it appeared wise to issue a warning at this stage lest it be assumed that this experience follows a fixed chronological pattern.

The Nature of Faith

We have seen that appreciation of Jesus' uniqueness is expressed in a relationship to us of immediacy and that recognition of it is made on the basis of faith. We have referred to the part that faith plays in the establishing of facts and to the common Christian conviction that faith owes its rise to the indwelling grace of God.

[11]Karl Barth, *The Doctrine of the Word of God*, part 1, trans. G. T. Thomson (vol. 1.1 of *Church Dogmatics*; Edinburgh: T. & T. Clark, 1936), p. 280.

[12]cf. Ephesians 2.8.

[13]Although McIntyre, after mentioning IG as a "corollary" of the understanding of revelation in the Old Testament, does not mention it again, it is clear that he would agree that it is a corollary in every revelational situation—including, of course, that pointed to in the New Testament.

We have now to discuss the nature of faith itself.

A complete discussion of "the dynamic and vital context of man's meaningful dependence upon the activity of God in Christ"[1] (which is one modern theologian's description of faith) would be long and widely-ranging; we shall therefore concentrate attention on the aspects which bear most upon the place of the historical Jesus.

This leads us to consider first the relationship of faith to its object and then the manner in which faith arises.

Mention of the terms "object" and "manner" leads naturally to the distinction sometimes made between *fides quae creditur* and *fides qua creditur*. We shall see how this distinction has arisen and what validity it has.

It does not require a very intimate acquaintance with the New Testament to discover that the word "faith" occurs there in more than one sense. Walter Bauer divides the occurrences into three classes:[2]

(a) Those referring to that which causes faith and trust: what we usually describe as "faithfulness" or "reliability". Of this use there are but few certain instances.

(b) Those referring to the act of "believing" in the religious sense: what we usually mean by "faith" or "trust". This class embraces the majority of the occurrences in the New Testament.

(c) Those referring to that which is believed: what we usually mean by a "body of belief" or "doctrine".

---

[1] John Dillenberger, in *A Handbook of Christian Theology*, ed. M. Halverson and A. A. Cohen (London: Fontana Religious Books, 1960), p. 131.

[2] Walter Bauer, *A Greek-English Lexicon of the New Testament and Other Early Christian Literature*, trans. W. F. Arndt and F. W. Gingrich (Cambridge: Cambridge University Press, 1957), pp. 668–70.

The last two are the senses which concern us here; and the occurrences of each are sufficiently numerous to make unnecessary the citation of them all. We mention only, as examples of the former: Mark 11.22 ("have faith in God"), Luke 18.42 ("your faith has made you well"), Romans 3.26 ("he justifies man on the score of faith in Jesus Christ"), and II Timothy 3.15 ("the sacred scriptures that can impart saving wisdom by faith in Jesus Christ"). Examples of the latter are: Galatians 1.23 ("is now preaching the faith he once destroyed") and Jude 3 ("the faith once delivered to the saints").

This two-fold connotation of the word "faith" suggests that even as early as the time of the New Testament there was some consciousness of a possible distinction to be drawn, yet with difficulty and perhaps only in theory, between that in which one has faith and the faith itself. It is the elaboration of the distinction between these two (as well as of their inter-relationship) which is represented by the terms *fides quae* and *fides qua*.

The distinction appears to have originated with Augustine, who wrote in *De Trinitate* (XIII.2): "*Aliud sunt ea quae creduntur, aliud fides qua creduntur*," while the seventeenth-century Lutheran, John Gerhard "was probably the first expressly to use the concepts . . . *fides quae creditur* and *fides qua creditur*, the first of which signifies the object of the second, the *materia circa quam*, the second the πεποίησις *et* πληροφορία in *animo credentis*."[3]

The distinction between these two may be useful for purposes of discussion but it is not one that can be held to finally, for each may be seen to presuppose

[3]So Karl Barth, *The Doctrine of the Word of God*, part 1, p. 270.

the other. Faith which is believed assumes someone who is the believer, and faith as it is believed assumes some object of belief. As Barth says:

> The distinction of *fides quae* and *fides qua* can obviously only have the meaning of signifying the dialectic of the object-subject content of the concept of faith, . . . the problem of faith and of the object of faith as such. To the discussion of this problem itself this distinction makes no contribution, for . . . all it would amount to would be to determine what is to be meant by *fides qua*.[4]

And concerning this *fides qua* Barth says in a later volume of his *Church Dogmatics*:

> New Testament faith does not curve in upon itself or centre on itself as *fides qua creditur*. The content of New Testament proclamation does not consist only of the description and reception of this *fides qua creditur*. Rather they relate to and are based upon a primary message concerning Jesus Christ himself, to which New Testament faith is open and has constantly to open itself, which must always be the first word of New Testament proclamation not only because in this message we have its historical starting-point, but because in it we have its origin and primary theme, because without it there cannot be those implicates, because this message is the thing which implies, without which anything we might say here about the being of man would be left hanging in the air, like a subsidiary clause which has no principal clause.[5]

[4]*ibid.*
[5]Karl Barth, *The Doctrine of Reconciliation*, part 1, trans. G. W.

Any proper understanding of *fides qua* sees it as pointing beyond itself to its object.

If we now apply what has been disclosed of this interrelationship to the situation in which the believing historian sees the historical Jesus as having the immediacy associated with his uniqueness we shall see that, though we may for the sake of clarity in discussion distinguish between the facts (the *fides quae*) and the activity of the historian who establishes them (the *fides qua*), there can be no ultimate separation of them, for each presupposes the other. A good deal of our earlier discussion has been directed towards making plain that there can be no facts apart from a historian establishing them.[6] The discussion here has made plain that there can be no historian without facts which he establishes, and there cannot be facts without events to which they relate.[7] This is important for understanding the nature of faith.

Our discussion of the relationship of faith to its object will be carried further by considering another classical conception: that which regards personal faith (*fides propria*) as composed of knowledge, assent and trust (*notitia, assensus* and *fiducia*).[8]

Bromiley (vol. IV.1 of *Church Dogmatics*; Edinburgh: T. & T. Clark, 1956), p. 248.

[6] There can of course be *events*, but events without facts are events of which the historian knows nothing at all.

[7] More accurately (since the possibility of wholly unbased facts must be conceded), we should say that every historian must have before him some data, by the interpretation of which he is establishing his facts, and that all data must be related to some event (even if the event be wholly fictitious).

[8] The Reformed statement of this conception is outlined by Heinrich Heppe, *Reformed Dogmatics*, rev. and ed. Ernst Bizer, trans. G. T. Thomson (London: George Allen & Unwin Ltd., 1950), pp. 530–4.

The element of trust is necessary, the Reformers said, because without it faith would be but a bare affirmation of certain things as true, without any appreciation of their calling for acceptance and decision.[9] Assent (not a theoretical but a practical one) is necessary, since it is by this that things are approved as true. And knowledge is necessary, since without it faith would have its only reality in the believing subject.[10]

Thus, while it was said by some that the essence of faith is *fiducia*, there was a firm recognition that this was not the only element.

To exclude from faith the element of *notitia* or *assensus*, i.e. the element of knowledge, to conceive of faith as pure trust, which is intellectually without form or, in view of its intellectual form, indifferent, as any kind of trust in any kind of thing, to make the object of faith problematic and to transfer the reality of faith to the believing subject, was a possibility of which we can say with certainty . . . that even in the early period of the Reformation none of its responsible leaders took it seriously for one single minute.[11]

No more can we take it seriously today. There can be no proper understanding of the nature of faith

[9]This was called *opinio* or *fides historica*, and is very much what many writers to-day have in mind when they speak of "historical knowledge" of Jesus, and what we earlier (p. 142) referred to as A. It is part of my aim in these pages to show that *x*A is as much historical knowledge of Jesus as is A, and indeed that *x*A is more a true historical knowledge of Jesus than A.

[10]Reformed theologians were also eager to point out that without *notitia* there would be but *fides implicita*, "by which we believe what the Church believes, without knowledge of the object of faith" (Johannes Wollebuis, *Christianae Theologiae Compendium* (1626), 139, cited by Heppe, *op. cit.*, p. 530.

[11]Karl Barth, *The Doctrine of the Word of God*, part I, p. 268.

which fails to see it as pointing beyond itself to its object.[12]

This disclosure of the way in which faith presupposes its object leads us to consider what this object is, and in what way it can be truly said that faith depends upon it.

We have already seen that the peculiarity of the relationship between Jesus and the believing historian involves the recognition of him not as A but as xA, and that this recognition is made on the basis of faith. We may therefore approach the question, "What is the object of faith?" by asking: "What is it that faith discerns?"

The answer must be: faith discerns Jesus himself—him of whom we said before, "his place in the historical process is to make known to all men the truth about their own place in it."[13]

We are speaking here of what many writers call the "event" of Jesus; and it is important to notice that it is an *event* in our specialized use of the word. It is made what it is at least in part by our response to it, and it is always beyond our complete comprehension.

At an earlier stage of our discussion[14] we saw how subsequent happenings can themselves be seen as part of an event and how even the historian himself, in his "response" to the event, becomes part of it. Having this understanding of the situation we can agree with R. H. Fuller when he says that the object of our faith is not the historical Jesus but "the Risen Christ

---

[12]While we have reached this point by means of discussing the three elements of *notitia, assensus* and *fiducia,* Barth does so by means of an analysis of the concept of *fiducia* alone (*ibid.,* pp. 268–70). What his discussion does is show the mutual interdependence of the three elements.

[13]*supra,* p. 134.   [14]*supra,* pp. 99-100.

preached by the Church". Our agreement is because Fuller goes on to say: "But the Risen Christ is in continuity with the historical Jesus, and it is the historical Jesus which makes the Risen Christ not just an abstraction but clothes him with flesh and blood."[15]

We have seen at several points that any event remains beyond complete comprehension. It is certainly the case that no man can know the event of Jesus in its fulness: each can but assemble all the data available to him, make the interpretation he sees to be best, and so establish the *fact*—and no fact can completely match the event.

It follows that there is truth in Kierkegaard's oft-quoted statement:

> The historical fact that the God has been in human form is the essence of the matter; the rest of the historical detail is not even as important as if we had to do with a human being instead of with the God. . . . If the contemporary generation had left nothing behind them but these words: "We have believed that in such and such a year the God appeared among us in the humble figure of a servant, that he lived and taught in our community and finally died", it would be more than enough.[16]

There is truth in this statement because any "historical detail" which it would be possible for the contemporary generation to leave behind would be what we have called a datum or (since no historian can

---

[15]G. Ernest Wright and Reginald H. Fuller, *The Book of the Acts of God; Christian Scholarship Interprets the Bible* (London: Gerald Duckworth & Co. Ltd., 1960), p. 193.

[16]Søren Kierkegaard, *Philosophical Fragments*, trans. David F. Swenson and Howard V. Hong, Second edition (Princeton: Princeton University Press, 1962), p. 130.

consider data without interpreting them) a fact;   it
could not in any circumstances be an event or complete
knowledge of an event.   And, as no amount of wrong
facts established by a historian can affect the substance
of the event itself, it is possible to say that the only
result of another historian's dismissal of those facts
one by one will be a clearer understanding of what
the event really was.

It follows also from our understanding that what
faith discerns is the event that the entertainment of
doubt concerning this or that detail of the New
Testament picture of Jesus need not greatly concern
the believer.   For all such details are part of the
picture because they are facts established by the
historians who wrote the New Testament;   the suggestion that some of these facts have been established
erroneously does not affect the reality of the event to
which they relate.

And it follows, thirdly, that the occurrence of faith
does not require a prior judgment on any historical
question.   A man can become immediately related to
Jesus, the event, without having established any
particular fact.   Nor need any preacher think that,
before he can present to the unbeliever the possibility
of enjoying the relationship of immediacy, he must
persuade him to accept as true this and that detail
of the New Testament picture.   Historiography is
not a necessary discipline for soul-culture or evangelism.

Here we recall our warning against assuming a fixed
chronological pattern for the occurrence of faith.   It
was said then that what we have in the recognition of
Jesus' immediacy is the transformation of A by x
which, as a new fact, leads the historian to see in a

new way all that had been previously established.[17]
This way of putting it may have given the impression
that the whole of what (*remota fide*, as it were) we
called A had to be established before *x* could make its
appearance. It was also said there,[18] however, that the
experience may follow a different order. A may be
known only in part when *x* enters the situation, or
there may never be a point at which A is not appreciated
as being *x*A.[19]

The position just advanced however cannot be left
entirely as it has been stated.

It is true that faith depends upon the event of Jesus
and not upon the facts which the historian establishes,
but these facts constitute the only knowledge he has
of the event. Unless therefore we are to say that the
believer need not know anything of that in which he
believes (and our discussion concerning faith's presupposition of its object has shown that we cannot
say that), we must recognize that after all facts are
somehow necessary to faith.

We could perhaps remark that no one has ever come
to faith without establishing some facts concerning
faith's object, and leave it at that. It will be useful
however to look again at the statements which were
made to support the contention that, faith's object
being the event, this and that fact can be done away
with and faith left undisturbed.

In Kierkegaard's well-known statement he does
not say that absolutely everything about Jesus can be
done away with: there must remain "the essence of

---

[17]*supra*, pp. 142-4.   [18] *supra*, p. 147.
[19]The questions whether *x* can precede A, and whether any precise
content can be predicated of A are considered *infra*, p. 158 and
pp. 159-60.

the matter"—namely, "the historical fact that the God has been in human form". And (even allowing for a difference in the use of the term) this is clearly a *fact* which the historian establishes concerning something which has happened in the past.[20] A similar conclusion must be drawn in respect of every attempt to treat as insignificant the details of any picture of the historical Jesus. It is true that no one of those details, and no construction of them all, can properly be regarded as the event itself, but there cannot be a removal of them *all* without the dismissal of the event itself. So long as it is known that an event took place the knower must have established some facts concerning it: the very nature of knowledge of the past makes that a *sine qua non*.

While it is true that every detail of the New Testament picture is a fact established by a historian and so not an integral part of the event, we cannot go on to say that all of the facts involved in the New Testament picture of Jesus can be dispensed with, and the historian still be left with some knowledge of the historical Jesus. For to obliterate the New Testament picture in that way means to obliterate also knowledge of the event.

Much the same treatment is to be accorded the statement that the occurrence of faith does not require a prior judgment on the historical question. The believer, it is true, does not always, or indeed often, first decide for or against certain historiographical positions and then allow faith to enter and transform

---

[20]For Kierkegaard the existence is the "fact" and the "essence of the matter". When he goes on to say that if we had only the testimony in a certain form "it would be more than enough", he does not mean a testimony devoid of historiographical support.

the situation. But neither does the believer have a faith devoid of reference to what he considers to be the true facts (and so as close an approximation to the event as he can make). Whatever be the chronological pattern of the experience, the continuing situation is one in which the believer knows xA, not xX,[21] and certainly not x alone. "How shall men believe in him of whom they have never heard?"[22]

This discussion has led us to the point where we seem to have made two contradictory assertions. We have said, on the one hand, that faith's object is the event of Jesus, and that it is not to be thought of as resting on any facts that we establish. On the other hand, we have said that faith cannot exist in the absence of facts that we establish. This evident contradiction calls for further consideration.

In complex situations of any kind it is very difficult to state, in a manner consonant with all the requirements of logic and definition, the precise boundaries of each factor and just what is its relationship to every other.

Now the situation which we are here discussing is an exceedingly complex one, wherein knowledge, assent and trust, thought, feeling and will, *fides qua* and *fides quae*, stand in an interdependency of relationship so intricate that it is only by an unusual, and somewhat artificial, effort of analysis that such distinctions as we have been discussing can be made.

In view of this complexity we must not be surprised if there emerge distinctions which we can indicate rather than delineate, and if in the course of our doing so we seem to utter contradictions.

[21]x, of course, here means something quite unknown.
[22]Romans 10.14.

The appearance of contradiction is diminished if, secondly, we recall how impossible it is for the historian to make an ultimate distinction between the event and the fact. He knows that the event and the fact are not to be identified but he does not know anything of the event save through the fact.

When therefore the Christian says that the object of his faith is the event of Jesus he is saying something that is true. But when he goes on to make the apparently contradictory statement that his faith rests on a fact which he knows about Jesus he is also saying something that is true, for his knowledge of the event is restricted to the fact.

Moreover, as Foster suggests, the Christian will consider the whole framework of conditions which determine where and what he is, at the moment of the act of faith, as part of the pattern of prevenient grace;[23] and he will on that account find it extraordinarily difficult to say of any one factor that it, and not another, is the real object or cause of his faith.

In the third place, not everything that may be present in the situation we are discussing (even if it could be shown to be necessary) has to be regarded as the *object* of faith. "By ground or basis of faith is not ordinarily meant whatever in fact has produced the situation in which we can have faith, but rather that to which faith in its own inward and essential structure must consciously point and cling."[24]

It remains in this discussion of the relationship between faith and its object to consider whether there is some *sine qua non* of knowledge of the object—in other words, whether there is some minimum know-

[23]A. D. Foster, *op. cit.*, p. 399.   [24]*ibid.*

ledge of A, the absence of which precludes the discerning of xA.

We have already seen that though faith does not depend upon any fact it does not arise in the absence of facts; and so the answer to our present question seems plain: some minimum knowledge of the object *is* required. The interrelationships of knowledge, assent and trust, of *fides qua* and *fides quae*, of event and fact, make that conclusion inescapable.

The *reductio ad absurdum* removes any remaining doubt on this point. Let us suppose that *every* fact which any believer has established concerning Jesus has been dismissed, so that he no longer retains even the fact of Jesus' existence: if that stage is reached there simply could not be faith in him.

It is one thing to be confident that there must be some essential minimum of knowledge; it is another to be confident about identifying its content. From any attempt to do so in a definitive way I abstain, offering only the suggestion that the minimum involves the facts that Jesus lived on our earth at some period in the past and that he was uniquely related to God.[25] No other facts, it seems to me, can be defined as *essential* for the emergence of faith, though a good deal of our discussion will have shown that I am far from suggesting that other facts are irrelevant to faith. It is extremely unlikely that the faith of any person has ever been associated with facts so meagre as those

---

[25]cf. what John Macquarrie says about "a minimum core of historical factuality which cannot be doubted". He defines this as: "that there was someone who once exhibited in history the possibility of existence which the *kerygma* proclaims. . . . Put into theological language, the minimal assertion is 'that the Word became flesh and dwelt among us', in one possible sense of this pregnant saying." *The Scope of Demythologizing*, p. 93.

which have just been suggested as the essential minimum; and it may be the case that this minimum is different for each individual. Certainly different people have come to faith with different facts, and it is quite impossible for us to determine whether anyone of them could have come to faith with a set of facts other than those he had.

Does the existence of such a minimum (however defined) set limits to the believer's practice of historiography? Are there some facts which, because faith could not exist without them, must never be questioned by the believer?

It will be easiest to discuss this in terms of the extreme case. Does his faith make it impossible for the Christian ever to raise the question of Jesus' existence?

No, it does not. It *is* possible for the Christian historian to consider the question of Jesus' existence since this is a fact established by historiographical enquiry, and his faith is not something which exists without regard for such facts. He may be led to consider the question because some critic has told him that his faith seems to rest on a fiction; he may be led to consider it because he is anxious to commend the Gospel in a way that shows that it welcomes intelligent enquiry into its postulates; he may be led to consider it because he is aware that faith can be nourished by the extension of *notitia* as well as of its other factors; and so on. Whatever the reason for taking it up, the Christian historian can give the question as proper consideration as any other historian. There is a measure of uncertainty attaching to every historical fact and the Christian historian cannot exclude it from the fact of Jesus' existence.

What, then, of the basis of faith? If even the essential minimum of A is uncertain, what sure status can be accorded xA?

The believing historian is in no doubt concerning the sure basis of his faith, not because his faith forbids him to make a proper historiographical enquiry, but because he is confident concerning the outcome of any proper enquiry.

His certainty on this score is due not only to such factors as "infinity of indirect references", which, as we saw,[26] give a practical certainty to facts which epistemological principles show to be uncertain— though, indeed, such factors abound in the case of Jesus. The believing historian's certainty is supported by the immediacy of relationship in which he stands to Jesus. Thus, as H. P. Owen says:

> When the Christian approaches Christ "objectively" through historical judgment he simultaneously approaches him "subjectively" through historic faith. Because the two approaches are simultaneous, the subjective certainty of faith is able to confer objective certainty upon evidence that would otherwise remain no more than probable.[27]

What the Christian historian must not do is assume that the fact he has established at any time is the final one, completely matching the event. Even the knowledge which faith assists is in need of growth and correction.

Thus Christian faith has no need to curtail the

[26]*supra*, pp. 111-12.
[27]H. P. Owen, *Revelation and Existence*, p. 129. In this passage Owen is using "historical" and "historic" in the senses which are ascribed in contemporary theological discussion to the German words *historisch* and *geschichtlich*, respectively. See *infra*, p. 173-5.

pursuit of historiography. On the contrary, there is every reason for encouraging it.

Faith cannot arise in the complete absence of facts concerning Jesus; and each believer must be concerned to ensure that the facts he holds arise from the most adequate interpretation possible of as many data as possible.

Even though there be some believers who would gain nothing from the pursuit of historiographical science,[28] it cannot be gainsaid that the Church as a whole has much to gain from its ardent pursuit by some or most of its members. Apart from benefits in the understanding of the object of faith (if not in the improvement of faith itself) which are bound to follow historiographical enquiry, there is the advantage of improved communication in proclamation of the Gospel as beyond suspicion when its statements are tested at the bar of historiographical research.[29] It is true that the historical question has loomed large in the last century or two while for eighteen hundred years the Gospel was believed in and preached with scarcely any regard for the matters which today are so widely canvassed. But strong Christian faith in every century has been related to such ideas of historiography as were current, and it must continue to be related to them.

There has long been a controversy between those who contend that faith can arise only as God takes

---

[28]"Historiographical science" is here used in the strict sense of the process of arriving at knowledge of the past, as that process is carried out by those especially skilled (*supra*, p. 20). Obviously, every believer must be an historian in the broad sense (*ibid.*) in order to have any facts at all concerning Jesus.

[29]cf. what was said on pp. 15–16 as a reason for regarding our topic as an important one.

the initiative, man having only a passive part, and those who contend that this attitude denies to man any power and responsibility of decision. In view of the part we have assigned to faith in the work of finding the historical Jesus we are bound to say something concerning the source of its occurrence.

At one point in this chapter we referred to the common Christian conviction that faith is a gift from God; and at a number of other points our presentation of the relationship between faith and knowledge has suggested that human decision is by no means an irrelevant factor. Thus we ourselves seem to be halting between the two opinions referred to in the last paragraph. On which side shall we stand? Or does the form of our presentation suggest that we shall stand on neither?

The antagonists in this controversy have tended to sharpen the issue between them in a way which overlooks a proper analysis of the faith experience itself. This experience is a paradoxical compound of man's act and God's, in a fashion which nowhere suggests that the more there is of one the less there must be of the other. D. M. Baillie has made this plain in his description of "the paradox of grace".[30] Brunner has characterized the divine command as both gift and demand[31] (*Gabe* and *Aufgabe*, as his language enables him to put it neatly). And Dillenberger writes:

> Faith as the gift of God is the confession of the
> believer that in his depths he knows the foundation

---

[30]D. M. Baillie, *God Was in Christ*, pp. 114–18.
[31]Emil Brunner, *The Divine Imperative; a Study in Christian Ethics*, trans. Olive Wyon (London: Lutterworth Press, 1937), pp. 114–21.

and source of his decision to be of God, that the decision itself is authentic, validating the self, precisely as it has been known to lie somewhere else than in the self. Hence, the priority of God can never be defined apart from the reception or the experience of God.[32]

If there is this polarity of God-given and man-decided in the experience of faith itself we need not be surprised that our presentation of the way in which knowledge of the historical Jesus is arrived at involves a parallel polarity of truth-as-given and truth-as-attained. As a matter of fact, such a polarity may be traced in arriving at historical facts of every kind, having its formal analogy in the *a priori* and the empirical elements of historical enquiry which we discussed earlier.[33]

The Faith of the Church

Thus far we have spoken of faith in the life (including the thinking) of the individual and have said nothing concerning the community of people who through the ages have had like faith and who together form the Christian Church. Yet it is important that we say something concerning this, for no individual's faith (therefore no Christian's picture of the historical Jesus) would be what it is without the Church.

No good purpose would be served by embarking here upon discussion of the many questions connected with the nature of the Church. It will be sufficient to think of the Church as embracing all in every age who have Christian faith. To this could be added:

[32]John Dillenberger, in *A Handbook of Christian Theology*, p. 132.
[33]*Supra*, p. 111.

"and who join themselves to some group of people recognized as Christians" since (leaving aside the question of how such recognition is to be made) practically all who have faith do join themselves to such a group, and those who fail to do so owe more to the group than they appreciate.

The existence of the Church is significant for understanding the nature of faith in at least three ways.

(a) The Church is the body which holds what may be called the "group-memory" of Jesus: that memory of the historical Jesus not possessed because any of the present[1] members of the Church shared his company in Galilee, but nonetheless a real memory of his influence on the thought and actions of the community as well as on its individual members.

This, according to C. C. J. Webb, is what we should have in mind when we speak of "the historical element in religion". It is, he says, "primarily a sense of continuity with the past of the religious community of which a man finds or makes himself a member, and through which, at any rate for the most part, his religious experience is mediated."[2] Earlier in the same book Webb writes:

> One cannot doubt that it is just in the sense of belonging to a community—tribe or family or voluntary brotherhood—which has a past not remembered by oneself, yet of which one is told by those who themselves remember it or have been in like manner told of it by others, that there first arises in the human mind that interest in the

[1] i.e. "present on the earth"; I do not suggest that the saints *in gloria* have ceased to be part of the Church.

[2] C. C. J. Webb, *The Historical Element in Religion* (London: George Allen & Unwin Ltd., 1935), p. 27.

past which is the presupposition of all history.[3]

The knowledge any man has of the historical Jesus owes something to what may be learned from the Church's memory of Jesus. To put this in another way, it owes something to the facts concerning Jesus which members of the Christian community have established—agreement upon which constitutes the bond holding them together. Using these facts as data, along with others, each man will establish facts of his own; but the man who pays no attention whatever to the information about Jesus provided by the Church forfeits any claim to have investigated the question adequately. This is true of both believer and unbeliever.

(b) The relationship of the individual to the Church is not one-sided; there is a reciprocity of interest and dependence. It is the existence of the Church, with its declaration of the uniqueness of Jesus and the possibility of an immediate relationship to him, which occasions the circumstances in which the individual's faith arises. It is the occurrence of faith in this individual and that, from generation to generation, which keeps the Church in existence.

To speak thus of a reciprocity between the individual and the Church is not to deny that there is an action which transcends both. Whatever else it may be and whatever other factors may accompany it, faith is a gift of God; it is IG which enables C to discern xA. Here we are stating the circumstances in which that gift is given; and always the Church is part of the situation. Though it is not in itself a sufficient condition it is a necessary one.

The possibility of someone's coming to faith simply

[3]*ibid.*, p. 16.

by reading the Scriptures does not confute the statement that the Church plays a necessary part. On the one hand, the Bible itself arose within the Church; its books, as Knox says, "are concerned with the contemplation and interpretation of realities within the community's experience, and survived just because the community as a whole recognized in them a setting forth of its own true and authentic life."[4] On the other hand, no one would ever read the Bible if the Church were not at work in the distribution and commendation of it.

The same sort of thing is to be said concerning every means by which men are brought to knowledge of Jesus: always the agency of others who are believers (in other words the Church) must be presupposed.

To understand the relationship between the individual and the Church as one of reciprocity is to avoid two distortions of the situation. There is a distortion which considers the Church to be absolutely prior to the individual, able to lay down a determinative exposition of what his faith is and implies. There is on the other hand a distortion which regards the individual as absolutely prior to the Church, able to go along the way of faith without regard for what the Christian community has to say. As Knox says, aligning each of these tendencies in an illustrative way with a contemporary denominational grouping:

> The Roman Catholic is mistaken in so far as he identifies "the Church" with his own hierarchy but he is not mistaken in putting the Church above the individual and insisting on the decisive part the Church must have in the interpretation of scripture. The Protestant, on the other hand, is

[4]John Knox, *Criticism and Faith*, p. 28.

not mistaken in emphasizing the role of the Spirit
in the interpretation of scripture, and in pre-
ferring the voice of the Spirit to the vote of some
bishops, but he is badly mistaken if he supposes
that when he speaks of the Spirit, he is not also
speaking of the Church.[5]

Nels Ferré mentions Knox among theologians who
begin with the exposition of the faith of the Church
but do not rely

wholly upon the descriptive approach whereby
the Church's interpretation of the faith becomes
determinative for mankind. Their methods are
rather *configurative* and demand also the subjective response of faith. All this means, however,
is that collective and personal experience are
combined.[6]

What the Church does is to mediate between (in the
strict sense of that phrase: it "brings together") Jesus
and the believer. The Church and the individual
have a reciprocity of interest and dependence.

(c) Among the patterns of historical analysis mentioned by Morris Cohen in his discussion of *The
Meaning of Human History* is that commonly referred
to as the "institutional".

The essence of this approach is the insistence that
man is an animal that learns ways of thinking,
feeling and doing and continues to act in these
learned ways. Institutions are human arrange-
ments through which this learning takes place and
through which learned forms of conduct are
maintained. Learning in this context is largely,

[5]John Knox, *op. cit.*, p. 79.
[6]Nels F. S. Ferré, *op. cit.*, pp. 29-30. The other theologians whom
Ferré has in mind are Karl Barth and Reinhold Niebuhr.

but not entirely, a product of teaching, of handing down the accumulated traditions of the past; in part, learning must always be an exploration of the hitherto uncharted possibilities whose outer limits lie far beyond the horizons that most of us see.[7]

To understand this is to have additional knowledge concerning the interrelationship of Church and individual. One aspect of the reciprocity of interest and dependence is that the Church communicates to the individual the truth concerning Jesus and then continues to give him some measure of assurance about the rightness of the facts he has established. Though the recurrence of *Athanasius contra mundum* may not be unknown, it is as a matter of fact very rare; and it is doubtful whether any man would long hold to a view if he found no one to encourage him in the belief that he is right. True, there is a danger that the acceptance of this attitude may, by a species of mob psychology, lead a man to declare right what all his investigation tells him is false. This danger is obviated, however, when it is remembered that the institutional pattern of historical analysis teaches that though learning does involve what the institution teaches, it involves also exploration of "hitherto uncharted possibilities", and that the proper approach to the particular institution we have in mind is the "configurative" one which demands the subjective response of faith.

What happens is that a person either grows up in, or joins himself to a company whose "group-memory" of Jesus he implicitly accepts—and then grows into, modifying in the course of his growth the picture which is first presented to him. In the terminology of

[7]Morris R. Cohen, *op. cit.*, p. 229.

Knox which we used at an earlier stage,[8] the individual comes to be part of the response which is still being made to the event of Jesus, and so part of the event itself.

To be a Christian is something that goes deeper than our ideas and confessions and deeper than our code of behaviour. It means our incorporation in a stream of history and in the redemptive events which determine that stream. It means belonging to a community whose members participate in a shared drama of the past, in a revelatory history. This is evidently more than a matter of having the cult story preached; it is a matter of sharing in the cult rite and in the total life of the cult community. To share in this *life* is to appropriate the revelation in just as real a sense as to hear it proclaimed.[9]

[8] *Supra*, pp. 99-100.
[9] Amos N. Wilder, *Otherworldliness and the New Testament*, p. 55.

IV

History, Myth and Truth

NO ONE GOES FAR in theological discussion today without touching questions which Rudolf Bultmann and others have raised with the proposal to remove the mythological framework in which the Kerygma is encased: a proposal which has had bestowed upon it the title of "demythologizing" (*Entmythologisierung*). To relate our own discussion to the controversy surrounding this proposal will not only relate it to what many regard as the most significant movement in contemporary theology; it will also afford, by concrete reference, a valuable reiteration and further development of some points.

According to one of the proposal's foremost exponents, the reason for the controversy lies in the fact that while both sides declare that the reality which underlies the Christian faith is a historical one, they mean by the term quite different things. "What one side understands as historical is for the other side not historical at all."[1] The one approach (that which finds support in the official statements of the churches) sees its primary task to be the establishment of the

---

[1] Friedrich Gogarten, *Demythologizing and History*, trans. N. H. Smith (London: S.C.M. Press Ltd., 1955), p. 10.

events described in the New Testament in their "objectivity" or "real factualness". The other approach (the one involved in the theology of demythologizing) arises from the conviction that their actual historical character is to be sought in "the proclamation and witness that in the events of this history God turns with grace towards mankind and their world".

On the one view, "history is understood . . . primarily as referring to past events and the task of the historian is taken to be the reconstruction of the past on the basis of documentary tradition."

On the other view, it is considered that "the study of history has not yet achieved its purpose when it has completed its investigative work of reconstructing and establishing the historical events of the past but that the purpose is fulfilled only with the historical interpretation of these facts as a possibility of human existence."[2]

The demythologizers appear therefore to be saying much that we have asserted in earlier chapters. We have made it plain that historiography can never result in pure objectivity, that the present situation of the historian is bound to affect the facts which his interpretation of the data establishes, and that the historian makes a response to the event which he is investigating.

We shall see whether our agreement with the demythologizers is complete on these points and whether we can agree with them in others of their assertions.

The Programme of Demythologizing

A good way to move towards understanding the

[2]*ibid.*, pp. 37–8.

programme of demythologizing is to note some terms used in discussion of it.

We should note, first, the distinction made between two German words both of which find translation in English as "history": *Historie* and *Geschichte*. *Historie* means the study of past events with a view to discovering in an objective, detached manner what actually happened. *Geschichte* on the other hand means the study of past events in such a way that the discovery of what happened calls for decision on our part.[1] Corresponding to these words and the distinction between them are the two adjectives, *historisch* and *geschichtlich*, the former referring to what can be established in an objective way by the generally accepted methods of historiographical science, and the latter to what, occurring in the past, has an existential[2] significance in the present. R. H. Fuller established the practice of translating *historisch* by "historical" or "past historical", and *geschichtlich*

[1]This distinction is not germane to the words as they are commonly used, but has been adopted for purposes of technical discussion. It appears to have originated with Martin Kähler whose *Der sogenannte historische Jesus und der geschichtliche biblische Christus* was published in 1892. Paul Althaus speaks of the contemporary *Kerygma-Theologie* as *"eine Wiederaufnahme und neue Begründung"* of Kähler's thesis. *Das sogenannte Kerygma und der historische Jesus* (Carl Bertelsmann Verlag, 1958), p. 10. Hugh Anderson points out how, influenced by Wilhelm Herrmann as well as Kähler, Bultmann retained the notion of the inseparability of Jesus and his message but transferred to the *historisch* a good deal of what Kähler meant by the *geschichtlich*. "The Historical Jesus and the Origins of Christianity", *Scottish Journal of Theology*, vol. XIII (1960), p. 116.

[2]The practice followed here is to use the word "existentialist" when the reference is to the philosophical movement known as Existentialism, and "existential" when the reference is to existence as such. "Existentialist" is thus the equivalent of the German *existential* and the French *existential*, while "existential" is the equivalent of the German *existentiell* and the French *existentiel*.

by "historic",[3] so that these are the translations that appear in any citations from the volume, *Kerygma and Myth*; but my own preference is for the translations suggested by John Macquarrie: "objective-historical" and "existential-historical".[4]

Let us see the relationships these terms have to some which we have been using.

There is the term "historical" as we have understood it in the phrase, "the historical Jesus". In our usage this denotes the facts at which we arrive by interpretation of the data. In the demythologizers' terms these facts may be either "objective-historical" or "existential-historical", depending on whether we see them as having existential significance for us today.

To speak in this way of the possibility of historical knowledge being "objective-historical" seems to conflict with our earlier contention that no knowledge of the past can be purely objective; but it need not do so. When knowledge of an event is said to be *historisch* it may be allowed that this knowledge includes that interpretation of data without which there would be no knowledge of anything; the emphasis is upon the detached nature of some historical enquiry, which does not see the facts it establishes as having any influence upon the historian's way of living. For example, a question whether the Battle of Hastings took place in 1066 or 1067 would have no bearing upon the way the historian lives (in other words, it would not be an existential question for him), and any fact

---

[3]See the Translator's Preface to H. W. Bartsch (ed.), *Kerygma and Myth; A Theological Debate,* trans. R. H. Fuller (New York: Harper Torchbooks, 1961), p. xii.

[4]John Macquarrie, *An Existentialist Theology* (New York: Harper Torchbooks, 1965), pp. 166, 171.

established in answer to this question would be an objective-historical one.

The demythologizers consider that there can be similarly objective-historical facts concerning Jesus; and we may concede that there are historians who fail to see any significance for their own living in what they establish concerning him. We may even concede that there are some facts concerning Jesus which are without existential reference for any historian. What may be questioned in the demythologizers' way of stating this distinction is the suggestion that our facts may be *either* objective-historical *or* existential-historical; there exists the possibility (to which we shall return later) of their being *both*.

But in regard to certain of the facts which bear upon Jesus there is no question of their being objective-historical: namely, those relating to what we spoke of earlier as his uniqueness. They are, like all facts, arrived at by interpretation of data, but, because the establishment of these facts puts the historian in an immediate relationship to the event, they have that vital existential reference which is the characteristic of the existential-historical.

To say that every fact relating to immediacy is an existential-historical one is not, however, to say that immediacy and being existential-historical are the same thing. For example, the Declaration of Independence is presumably an existential-historical fact for every American (it certainly has reference to his life today), but it does not bear upon him as does the immediacy of Jesus upon the believer. We may go so far as to say that the historian may establish existential-historical facts concerning Jesus himself (as, for example, the fact that his teaching is largely responsible for the ethical code accepted by the community in which the historian lives) without there being any immediacy of relationship between Jesus and the historian.

That in Bultmann's view there can be existential-historical facts which do not relate to Jesus is made plain in a few pages of his Gifford Lectures.[5] In a discussion there of "objectivity in historical science" he shows that, in regard to a historian's judgment on *any* event, there is involved the choosing of a viewpoint and that in this choice there is involved "the existential encounter with history". Similarly, in his earlier "A Reply to the Theses of J. Schniewind", he speaks of "the historian's personal encounter with the past", which takes place "by his encountering in those events of the past (as his own history) human existence and its interpretation". He then adds:

With the recollection of the Kerygma it is other-wise. This does not present us with facts of the past in their bare actuality, nor does it lead to encounter with human existence and its interpre-tation, but, as a sacramental event, it represents the events of the past in such a way that it renews them, and thus becomes a personal encounter for me.[6]

Thus what we have spoken of as the facts relating to the immediacy of Jesus are, for Bultmann, certainly not objective-historical; nor can they be wholly described by calling them existential-historical; they are characterized by a uniqueness which distinguishes them from other facts of an existential-historical kind. Our own conclusion was that the facts relating to

[5]Rudolf Bultmann, *History and Eschatology*, pp. 117–19.
[6]*Kerygma and Myth*, p. 115.

the uniqueness of Jesus are facts arrived at in the same way as all historical facts; and we have not dismissed the possibility of their being *both* existential-historical *and* objective-historical.

Another term of which we must take account is "mythological".

Oddly enough, although it is this term which has given the name to his programme, Bultmann does not make quite clear what he means by it; and he is to be criticized on the score of ambiguity in his terminology if not on that of ambiguity in the conception itself.[7]

In a footnote to the essay which initiated the demythologizing controversy,[8] Bultmann says that he is using myth in the sense popularized by the "History of Religions" school. "Mythology is the use of imagery to express the other worldly in terms of this world and the divine in terms of human life, the other side in terms of this side."[9]

As he has expressed himself there Bultmann might

---

[7]cf. John Macquarrie's discussion of the four main lines along which Bultmann's handling of his key-term has been criticized. *The Scope of Demythologizing* (New York: Harper & Row, 1960), pp. 198–215. Macquarrie concludes that, though in various places Bultmann comes to grips with the questions raised in these objections, he made a mistake in introducing too rigid a definition at too early a stage in the discussion. *ibid.*, p. 201.

[8]"Offenbarung und Heilsgeschehen", published 1941 in *Beiträge zur Evangelischen Theologie*. Later this essay was published in two parts: "Die Frage der natürlichen Offenbarung" (*Glauben und Verstehen, Gesammelte Aufsatze*, vol. II, 1952); "Neues Testament und Mythologie" (*Kerygma und Mythos*, vol. I, ed. H. W. Bartsch (Hamburg: Herbert Reich, 1948). Both parts are available in English: "The Question of Natural Revelation" (R. Bultmann, *Essays Philosophical and Theological*, trans. J. C. G. Greig (London: S.C.M. Press Ltd., 1955), pp. 90–118); "New Testament and Mythology" (H. W. Bartsch (ed.) *Kerygma and Myth*, trans. R. H. Fuller (New York: Harper Torchbooks, 1961), pp. 1–44).

[9]H. W. Bartsch (ed.), *Kerygma and Myth*, p. 10.

be understood as suggesting that every attempt to describe divine activity in human language, or even to think of it by human minds, must be mythological, and the conclusion drawn that he does not want us to say anything about God at all. But the whole tenor of his initial essay and of much else that he has written shows that he considers it possible to speak of divine activity in terms which are not mythological. He says, for instance, that in his programme there still survive traces of mythology "for those who regard all language about God or of a decisive eschatological event[10] as mythological", but adds that "this is not mythology in the traditional sense, not the kind of mythology which has become antiquated with the decay of the mythical world view."[11]

Bultmann's criteria of the "mythological" are seen to be two. A concept is mythological (in the sense of requiring to be "demythologized") if it belongs to an obsolete cosmology, or if it expresses what is not true.

The first of these criteria does not need much discussion, for Bultmann makes it very plain that the proclamation of the Kerygma today simply cannot be in the categories which were accepted unquestioningly by Christians (and non-Christians) of the first century as descriptive of the world in which they lived. The first eight pages of his "New Testament and Mythology" are taken up with showing that the cosmology which regards the world as a "three-storied structure" and the earth as "more than the scene of natural, every-day events"[12] is obsolete, while his "Conclusion"

---

[10]Bultmann does not use "eschatological" in the sense of relating to a future *eschaton*. By an "eschatological event" he means "translation into an unworldly existence or, in New Testament language, being in Christ." (*Kerygma and Myth*, p. 113).
[11]*ibid.*, p. 43.   [12]*ibid.*, p. 1.

includes the remark that the kind of mythology which
he is concerned to do away with is that "which has
become antiquated with the decay of the mythical
world view."[13] This conception of the world is called
mythological, he has said elsewhere, "because it is
different from the conception of the world which has
been formed and developed by science since its
inception in modern Greece and which has been
accepted by all modern men."[14]

To use the word "mythological" in this way,
denoting what has become obsolete in thought about
the world generally, is to use it in a way found sometimes in common speech. But it is to use it somewhat
inaccurately and, moreover, in a way not wholly
consonant with the definition of mythology which
Bultmann himself has given. Yet it is plain that he
does use it in this way; and we have to take note of
it if we are to appreciate his meaning.

The second way in which Bultmann uses the term
"mythological" is to denote a concept expressing what
is not true.

It is obvious that any question of truth which
arises in connection with Bultmann's conception of
myth cannot be the question whether its imagery is
to be taken literally. "The real purpose of myth," he
says, "is not to present an objective picture of the
world as it is, but to express man's understanding of
himself in the world in which he lives." He says
further: "The real question is whether this understanding of existence is true."[15] That is to say, the

---

[13]*ibid.*, p. 43.
[14]R. Bultmann, *Jesus Christ and Mythology* (New York: Charles
   Scribner's Sons, 1958), p. 15.
[15]*Kerygma and Myth*, pp. 10–11.

question of the "truth" of the myth, as an objective description, does not arise at all. If it is an objective description it is not a myth.

The description "mythological" becomes appropriate when the imagery used "to express the other worldly in terms of this world" is not recognizable by men as a faithful expression of what they experience or can experience—in other words, when the imagery of a myth does not express for a man an "understanding of himself in the world" which is true. When on the other hand the imagery used *does* express what men experience (even if the understanding of its bearing on one's life here and now is not on the level of consciousness),[16] we are no longer in the realm of mere mythology; we have in fact a demythologized expression of the experience.

A few examples of the way in which Bultmann applies this criterion of truth will make the point clearer.

Having indicated that because man's radical self-assertion blinds him to the fact of sin, he regards sin as mythological, Bultmann goes on to say: "Sin ceases to be mere mythology when the love of God meets man as a power which embraces and sustains him in his fallen, self-assertive state."[17] That is to say, the man to whom the love of God has been revealed recognizes as a true description what he had previously regarded as mythological. To put it another way, the notion of the love of God coming from the "other world" into "this world" is not mythological if it is known as a reality in experience.

This idea of truth as a criterion of whether any particular form of expression is mythological appears

[16] *Jesus Christ and Mythology*, p. 74.   [17] *ibid.*, p. 31.

again when Bultmann indicates, in his reply to
Schniewind, that the belief that "man must be ready
to sacrifice to the deity what is dearest to him" is
not mythological until "the moment it ceases to be
controlled by a true conception of God."[18]

It also comes out clearly in what Bultmann says of
the Cross and the Resurrection.[19] "While it is beyond
question that the New Testament presents the event
of Jesus Christ in mythical terms," and "the crux of
the matter lies in the Cross and the Resurrection,"
"in its redemptive aspect the Cross of Christ is no
mere mythical event." For the man who has seen its
"cosmic significance", the Cross is a "permanent
fact rather than a mythological event". And the
Resurrection, which looks like "a mythical event pure
and simple", and which forms with the Cross "a
single, indivisible cosmic event" is not "a mythical
event like the resuscitation of a corpse", not "a mythological event adduced in order to prove the saving
efficacy of the Cross", but an article of faith. To
put this another way: the idea of Jesus' death as
"the judgment and salvation of the world" and of the
Resurrection as proclaiming this is not mythological
if it is known as a reality in experience.

"Those who regard all language about an act of
God as mythological" may insist that there is still
in this description of experience an element of myth
which ought to be removed, but, for Bultmann, this
description is not "mythological" because he believes
that such an apprehension of Jesus Christ as an event
of redemption does really take place. The fact that
it is a true description means that there is no call for
demythologizing at this point. "The language of myth,

⁸*ibid.*, p. 108.   ¹⁹*ibid.*, pp. 34–41

when it serves as the language of faith, loses its mythological sense."[20]

Underlying both these connotations of "mythological" is Bultmann's dislike of any suggestion that
God can be treated as an object. It is clear that such a
suggestion pervades the images we have just considered (or at least some forms of expressing them).
The same fault is to be found in the old cosmology
for there again God was dealt with as one thing among
others in an objectively describable universe. Bultmann maintains:

> Only such statements about God are legitimate
> as express the existential relation between God
> and man. Statements which speak of God's
> actions as cosmic events are illegitimate, . . .
> The so-called images which describe God as acting
> are legitimate only if they mean that God is a
> personal being acting on persons.[21]

One may remark incidentally that modern man's
inability to accept the old cosmology does not play
as large a part in calling for a demythologizing as the
presentation in Bultmann's initial essay suggests. If
it is wrong to "objectify" God, it must have been so
always; and it seems that Bultmann used the pre-
dicament in which modern man finds himself as a
device to draw attention to a need which in fact is
rooted more deeply.

> The task of demythologizing received its first
> impulse from the conflict between the mytho-
> logical views of the world contained in the Bible
> and the modern views of the world which are
> influenced by scientific thinking,

he writes, but adds:

[20]ibid., p. 67.   [21]ibid., pp. 69–70.

and it has become evident that faith itself demands to be freed from any world-view produced by man's thought, whether mythological or scientific. ... The criticism of the mythological world-view of biblical and ecclesiastical preaching renders a valuable service to faith, for it recalls faith to radical reflection on its own nature.[22]

With these terms understood we are better able to see what the demythologizers have in mind. It is their desire to remove from the Kerygma (as never having been an essential part of it) all that does not express, in terms understandable by men today, an experience which can be repeated in their own lives.

This does not mean, as may seem at first sight, that all facts relating to the immediacy of Jesus are to be condemned as mythological for, as we have seen, Bultmann and his followers recognize that the apprehension by men today of this immediacy is a possibility for their existence. What it does mean is that the only facts concerning the immediacy which can be accepted are existential-historical ones.

Another way of putting this is to say that all true facts concerning the redemptive act of God in Jesus are existential-historical; and that is not very different from saying that the facts relating to his immediacy are discerned by faith. Thus the demythologizers seem to be saying what we have ourselves been contending; but we must again sound a warning against concluding too readily that what is existential-historical may not also be objective-historical.

[22]*ibid.*, p. 83.

The Historical Basis for Faith

We are now in a position to look more closely at what the demythologizers mean when they say that the reality underlying the Christian faith is a historical one. This will be done by following in some detail the presentation made by Friedrich Gogarten, using Neville Horton Smith's translation, which includes certain changes and omissions made by the author.[1]

Smith translates both *historisch* and *geschichtlich* by "historical", but the result is not as confusing as might be expected. For one thing, the sort of distinction which we have indicated[2] between these two words is not made by everybody, even in German, and it is not made by those holding to the first of the views which Gogarten discusses. And in any case, where this distinction is relevant, the meaning to be attached to "historical" can be gathered from the context.

Let us consider first the view which is "broadly speaking the view held by the governing bodies of the Churches and the theologians connected with them."[3] An example of this view (though it is not one to which Gogarten refers) may be seen in the Declaratory Statement which forms part of the Basis of Union of the Presbyterian Church of Australia,[4]

---

[1]*Entmythologisierung und Kirche* (Stuttgart: Friedrich Vorwerk Verlag, 1953). E. T. *Demythologizing and History* (London: S.C.M. Press Ltd., 1955).

[2]*supra*, p. 173-5.

[3]Gogarten, *op. cit.*, p. 39. His examination of this view is in chapter VII (pp. 39–47).

[4]The whole Statement is printed in *Constitution and Procedure and Practice* (Melbourne: Board of Religious Education, 1950,)

where it is said that "the Christian faith rests upon, and the Christian consciousness takes hold of certain objective supernatural historic[5] facts".

The crucial difficulty is that on the one hand it must affirm "historical factualness" by which it means the same sort of historicity as historical science generally predicates of the occurrences it establishes (in terms of the Declaratory Statement, the facts are "objective"), and on the other hand affirm that these events are not after all just the same as other historical occurrences (in terms of the Declaratory Statement, these facts are "supernatural"). To the question, "How can this 'objective reality' be combined with 'the reality which cannot be established by historical means' in such a way that they are one and the same?" this view gives no sort of answer.

Gogarten considers that a certain sense can be found in all these assertions only if it is realized that unconsciously and probably involuntarily the argument is based on a medieval way of thinking which saw earth and heaven, time and eternity, man and God, natural and supernatural, as parts together of one general reality. It is however a way of thinking which has to an increasing extent been broken up by application of the historical method: whereas in the older view history is a process within a stationary world

---

pp. 21–3. The Basis of Union was agreed to on 24th July, 1901, when Presbyterian Churches of the six States united to form the Presbyterian Church of Australia. The Declaratory Statement has obvious affinities with the Declaratory Statement of the United Presbyterian Church of Scotland (1879) and the Declaratory Act of the Free Church of Scotland (1892).

[5]Of course, the use of this word here does not reflect the "historic"-"historical" distinction referred to *supra*, pp. 173-5.

and man's place is to adapt himself in accordance with its pre-established order, modern historiographical procedures show man to be himself responsible for history. The only difference, Gogarten says, between the medieval view of the faith and the view under discussion is that "in the former case it was a question of human and divine nature, of the natural and the supernatural, whereas here it is a question of the historical and the suprahistorical."

The case is no better if it is pointed out that in the assertion, "faith, as faith, knows itself to be supported and substantiated by facts", the reference is not to "facts" in their pure "objective factualness" but to a "supernatural reality" which, independently of faith, has given rise to faith as such and which "only faith indeed, as faith, perceives and recognizes in its objective factualness, from which faith as faith draws its life and nourishment, but which for all that is still factual reality". The case is no better because this too is a concept of reality genuine only for the metaphysical theology of the ancient Church and not for a historical theology. Once one has begun to think historically one must also think in historical terms of the reality with which faith is concerned.

Let us pause for a moment to recapitulate what Gogarten has said about this view, expressing his meaning in terms which we have ourselves employed in earlier chapters and relating his remarks particularly to the main topic of our discussion—the historical Jesus.

This view does not recognize the historian as properly playing any part in the establishment of facts (which are on this view identical with events); the historian's role is simply to note what they are. It declares that all the facts concerning Jesus (those related to his uniqueness or immediacy as well as those not so related) are to be discerned in the same way, and that those related to his uniqueness or immediacy are facts which only the believer discerns. This twofold assertion makes sense only if events which take place on our earth (or in our history) and those which take place in eternity are thought of as being of the same kind. Such a unitary view (a "peculiar combination of historical and metaphysical thinking"), Gogarten says, is impossible for anyone who recognizes himself to be part of historical occurrence.

The other view of the historical reality which underlies the Christian faith (the view involved in the theology of demythologizing) takes up the question which the first view fails to answer; that is to say, it seeks to define in historical terms the reality which, in the other theory, where it is conceived to be "supernatural" or "suprahistorical", necessarily remains outside history.

To appreciate what Gogarten has to say in exposition of this view[6] we must notice what he says earlier in his book concerning the nature of historical thought generally.

The modern historical method, he says, leads to a *Weltanschauung* which refers not only, or even primarily, to the understanding of the past; it is the expression of a realization that the whole world is man's world—no longer in the sense that he is to adapt himself in accordance with its pre-established order (this was the medieval view) but his in the sense

[6]Gogarten's exposition of this view is in chapter VIII of his book (pp. 48–81).

that it is for him to watch over it and provide it with form and order.

Man himself now becomes the fundamentally historical being who does not merely "himself creatively render possible his own outlook on life and the world", but also, by his historical decisions in politics, religion, cultural matters, economics, technology and the rest, gives the world the particular form in which it makes possible for a man a life that is in accordance with his human character. This change in the relation of a man to his world implies that all reality has now become historical for him. All that is real for us after this change is that which we are able to understand historically. And this means that metaphysical thinking has lost its position of dominance.[7]

Whereas history, in the sense in which it is still generally understood, is thought of as being principally concerned with what is past, and the attitude proper to the historian as that of a detached spectator, the approach which has been scientifically developed in recent times holds that such an objective attitude is not possible because the approach is itself historical.[8] In this view of history

the historical character of human existence is expressed in the concept of a responsibility which can be fulfilled only with man's being. This concept implies that man stands with respect to the world in a relation in which he stands originally, that is to say a relation in which he stands already and has always stood, and not a relation which he must establish only subsequently as an

[7]*ibid.*, p. 26.   [8]*ibid.*, p. 27.

isolated subject, as was the case within the subject-object pattern of thought, by either proving or "believing in" the reality of the world.[9] Man is not thought of as the subject which is confronted by history as an object; man is himself historical, and cannot in any way take himself out of history. Thus the crucial problem of history is that of an interpretation which approaches history not from the outside but from within the historical character of human existence.[10]

This is the view of history according to which those who hold the theology of demythologizing claim that their assertion, "Christ the Crucified and Risen One comes before us in the Word of the proclamation and nowhere else", is not, as their opponents have asserted, a denial of the Cross and the Resurrection as redemptive facts of a history which has taken place. In their view the Kerygma does have the character of history and in the existentialist interpretation of the New Testament message there is no "collapse of the bridge between the historical Jesus and the preached Jesus."[11]

---

[9]*ibid.*, p. 52.

[10]*ibid.*, pp. 57–8. Gogarten devotes several pages (pp. 57–65) to expounding Heidegger's understanding of the nature of history. As against the common idea of the world, and indeed all that is, as the object which man envisages, he holds that conception is "unconcealing oneself for. . . ." (*das Sich-entbergen für.* . . .); it is "perception of that which is present, to the 'unconcealedness' (*Unverborgenheit*) of which perception itself pertains as a particular kind of presence (*Anwesen*) in relation to the unconcealed 'that which is present' " (p. 65). What is thus true in general of "what is" is true also of history or of that which is historical and of the understanding of it (p. 65): an event "un-conceals" (*ent-birgt*) itself in history, and this event which un-conceals itself is to be perceived only by means of a corresponding "self-un-concealment" on the part of him for whom or to whom it happens (p. 81).

[11]*ibid.*, pp. 66–8.

in any present apprehension of the existential-historical free ourselves entirely from the results of objective-historical investigation.

Ronald W. Hepburn writes:

An event such as a piece of prophetic symbolism may be historical (Jesus did enter Jerusalem in triumph, did curse the fig tree) and at the same time be mythological in Bultmann's sense. Or the alleged event may not have happened and the narrative still retain mythological value. What one must insist is that whether or not the imagery, etc., of the narrative yields itself to translation into existentialist terms, this does nothing to tell us which of those possibilities is more likely to be true. Yet Bultmann repeatedly suggests that, "X is described in mythological terms" implies "X cannot have happened as narrated", and does not make it plain that the latter judgment requires a quite distinct investigation.[24]

Hepburn is right in distinguishing these two factors, but wrong in thinking that either can be the subject of "quite distinct investigation". The historian for whom an event is existentially significant cannot establish his facts as if this were not so; nor can the significance be precisely the same whether he believes the event to have happened in this way or that.

There are, as H. P. Owen remarks, (at least) two possible responses to an event.

Let us suppose a Christian is confronted with Christ's teaching about forgiveness, either in a sermon or in his own reading of the New Testa-

[24]"Demythologizing and the Problem of Validity", *New Essays in Philosophical Theology*. Ed. Antony Flew and Alasdair MacIntyre (London: S.C.M. Press Ltd., 1955), p. 235.

Again we shall recapitulate what Gogarten has said, expressing his meaning in terms which we have employed.

This view declares that the historian is himself part of the sequence of events which make up history, so that he cannot regard events as an objective past of which he is a disinterested beholder; the data presented to him call for interpretation on his part, and his responsibility for making decisions can be met only as his whole being is involved in the interpretation. The facts concerning Jesus which are interpreted in this way are the historical reality which underlies Christian faith.

It is clear that this view of historical occurrence has a good deal in common with our own understanding of it. We have recognized that the historian has a part to play in acquiring knowledge of the past, and have spoken of his relationship to a past event being part of the response to it; indeed he is in a sense part of the event itself.[12] We have said also that what the historian himself is contributes to his knowledge of the event,[13] so that the believer's knowledge of, and response to the redemptive event is made what it is because of his faith;[14] all that he knows of the redemptive event on which his faith rests is the fact that he himself establishes.

There are nonetheless certain points at which we must regard the demythologizers' view of the historical as unsatisfactory. They centre about something at which we have already hinted: the assumption that if a fact is objective-historical it cannot be existential-historical (and *vice versa*). This assumption shows itself in three ways.

[12]*supra*, p. 99-100.   [13]*supra*, pp. 115-18.   [14]*supra*, pp. 142-6.

In the first place, so much emphasis is laid upon the "presentness" of the existential-historical that insufficient regard is had for the "pastness" which is also an essential part of it.

Bultmann is not without a recognition that this feature of "pastness" has a place. "I am surprised," he writes, "how readily people conclude that my interpretation of the New Testament eschatology implies a timeless 'now'."[15] He acknowledges that the New Testament claims that "faith only became possible at a definite point in history in consequence of an event,"[16] that "in its redemptive aspect the Cross of Christ is . . . a permanent historical fact originating in the past historical event which is the crucifixion of Jesus,"[17] and that what is "for faith . . . an ever-present reality" is "the unique event of the past."[18] But such acknowledgement of the element of "pastness" does not prevent Bultmann from unduly disparaging it. This arises not only from his anxiety to give full weight to the event as an ever-present reality[19] but also from his conviction that historiographical investigation can lead only to knowledge of a phenomenon of past history, not to knowledge of the event of redemption itself.[20] What I am contending by way of criticism is that, whatever be the soundness of Bultmann's motives for doing so, his disparagement of the "pastness" leads to a misrepresentation of what the existential-historical really is. Richard R. Niebuhr says: "The basic weakness of Bultmann's method is that it mistakes the transcendence of the past event for inertia. *Historie* is dismissed, as though it were not

[15]H. W. Bartsch (ed.) *Kerygma and Myth*, p. 114.   [16]*ibid.*, p. 22.
[17]*ibid.*, p. 37.   [18]*ibid.*, p. 110.   [19]*ibid.*, p. 110.
[20]*ibid.*, p. 117.

from *Historie* that the multiple interpretations of the Christian community gained their life and life-giving energies."[21]

The assumption that a fact cannot be objective-historical as well as existential-historical shows itself, secondly, in Bultmann's failure to take sufficient account of our involvement in the relativity of the historical process. What is present arises out of what is past and we who are in this present situation are ourselves what we are, at least in part, because of what has gone before. Schniewind writes:

Bultmann's definition of the historic in terms of decision and encounter actually demands a linear conception of time. Each event is connected with other events before and after. The moment it has happened it necessitates further decisions. Despite the incalculable and personal (as opposed to mechanical) character of decision, both decision and event imply a time-process rather than an immediate and unconditional present.[22]

And when Bultmann says, in an attempt to answer this line of criticism:

I am deliberately renouncing any form of encounter with a phenomenon of past history, including an encounter with the Christ after the flesh, in order to encounter the Christ proclaimed in the Kerygma, which confronts me in my historic situation.[23]

he shows clearly a refusal to allow that what is existential-historical can also be objective-historical.

Thirdly, Bultmann overlooks the fact that we cannot

[21]Richard R. Niebuhr, *Resurrection and Historical Reason*, p. 145.
[22]H. W. Bartsch (ed.), *Kerygma and Myth*, p. 82.
[23]*ibid.*, p. 117.

ment . . . He may say: "Yes, I see; Christ's view is right; this is how I ought to behave." Or he may use the language of encounter and say: "This is a command which God is addressing to me; I must obey it."[25]

Owen goes on to make three comments: that both responses can lead to a decision, that Bultmann has no right to expect that every one is equally capable of experiencing an encounter and that in any case the first response enjoys ontological priority over the second.

It is valuable to have pointed out that there may be these two responses but Owen is as mistaken as Bultmann in regarding them as essentially different. The first is as much "encounter" as the second:[26] it too has an existential significance. It may be that different people choose different ways of expressing the effect which the teaching of Jesus has had upon their lives. It may be too, as Owen suggests, that the image of encounter is more congenial to the German than to the British temperament.[27] Whether

---

[25]H. P. Owen, *Revelation and Existence* (Cardiff: University of Wales Press, 1957), p. 65.

[26]Unless we suppose that the Christian in the first case does not intend to do anything about behaving in the way that he recognizes as proper.

[27]cf. the remarks of another British theologian on the idea of revelation as "personal communication": "On the face of it, it suggests that God must speak to us somewhat as we speak to one another. But this obviously does not happen . . . Neither out of the scripture I read nor in the prayers I tried to make did any mental voice address me . . . no 'other' stood beside me, no shadow of presence fell upon me . . . And this is why, when Germans set their eyeballs and pronounce the terrific words, '*Er redet dich an*', I am sure indeed that they are saying something, but I am still more sure that they are not speaking to my condition." Austin Farrer, *The Glass of Vision* (Westminster: Dacre Press, 1948), cited in *Scottish Journal of Theology*, vol. IV (1951), p. 421.

the first of the responses mentioned by Owen is ontologically prior to the second may be doubted; what is certainly true is that the second response cannot be made without some appreciation of the content of the teaching. In other words, there cannot be an existential response which does not involve objective-historical knowledge.

The point may be illustrated from that extreme case to which we have referred before. The believer may remain unconcerned while historians argue concerning some details of the life of Jesus; but he would be very much concerned if the historians concluded that Jesus had never lived at all. In that case the believer would be compelled to answer the historians by showing that their findings were faulty; and to do that would be to engage himself in historiographical research thus making plain that there can be no independence of existential-historical facts from those established by objective-historical means.

In these ways there is evidenced a failure to accept the possibility that a redemptive fact may be both existential-historical and objective-historical. Such an attitude arises naturally from the concern which Bultmann and his followers feel at any suggestion that God can be treated as an object along with other objects.[28]

We agree that this is a very proper concern but not with the premise that what is known in existential encounter loses the significance it may have as an object of investigation independent of encounter. Earlier we spoke of the way in which one new fact can transform a mass of old ones without causing them to be discarded altogether,[29] and this is the case in

[28]*supra*, p. 183.   [29]*supra*, pp. 143-4.

regard to our knowledge of God and his ways. It may be agreed that God is not an object like other objects and that none can know him or his ways apart from an existential encounter which has no possible parallel. But God's encounter with us is in this world of space and time and it takes the form of an immediacy which is mediated.[30] Thus the Christian's understanding of Jesus as the revelation of God is not an understanding paying no attention to what may be known of Jesus by way of historiography;[31] the Kerygma's identification of the historical Jesus with the heavenly Lord[32] is not a mistake.

The demythologizers' failure to have sufficient regard for what must underlie the events proclaimed as the Kerygma is another point at which we must regard their view as unsatisfactory.

It is true that some people, considering the events of the life of Jesus, never perceive anything different from a myriad of other events which have occurred. For such people the facts are objective-historical or, if they are existential-historical in the sense that they have some existential significance for the historian, they are not possessed of that peculiar quality of existential-historicity which is associated with the relationship of immediacy to Jesus.[33]

Thus it is possible to have a knowledge of Jesus which is not a knowledge of his immediacy; not all who investigate his life become Christians.[34] The demythologizers are right to insist that the establishment of innumerable facts about Jesus is not in itself the same thing as knowing the event of redemption which he is.

[30]*supra*, pp. 137-9.   [31]*supra*, p. 144.   [32]*supra*, p. 146.
[3]*supra*, pp. 176-8.   [34]*supra*, pp. 140-7.

The point however (as we have already said in several connections) is that those who do perceive Jesus as having existential significance do not have this perception regardless of what may be known about him as an objective-historical phenomenon. The disciples of Jesus did not proclaim as Lord and Saviour one of whom they had no knowledge; it was Jesus of Nazareth, of whose sayings and deeds they knew, whom they proclaimed in this way; and it is difficult to believe that they found no basis for their proclamation in what they knew of his life. John Macquarrie writes:

> It appears to me that as soon as the historian admits the objective-historical reality of the figure of Jesus, he must also admit that he was a big enough figure to found the Christian religion— or to put the same thing in another way, he must recognize an objective-historical which can support the weight of the existential-historical. That is not to say, of course, that every incident recorded about Jesus must be objective fact, but it does argue that there must be a greater degree of continuity between the Jesus of history and the Jesus of faith than Bultmann seems willing to allow.[35]

A further weakness in the demythologizers' view of history is disclosed in the assumption that it can distinguish what in fact cannot be distinguished.[36]

Although Bultmann says that there are attempts at

---

[35] John Macquarrie, *An Existentialist Theology*, p. 180.
[36] This point, along with some others not so immediately relevant to our present discussion, is made in my article, "Evangelism, Mythology and Bultmann", *Canadian Journal of Theology*, vol. VI (1960), pp. 42–52.

demythologizing within the New Testament itself,[37] I do not think there is a single passage in which a distinction between what he calls the existential-historical and what he calls the mythological is obvious; indeed, the nature of Bultmann's call for a demythologizing, and the controversy which has ensued, are evidence that such a distinction is difficult to make. The writers of the New Testament did not feel that they had done their work when they had narrated a series of events, however unusual they considered these events to have been. They considered their narration of these events, if not the events themselves, to be incomplete unless their readers entered into an experience on the basis of them.[38] And it is doubtful whether the writers expected a full understanding of these happenings from any who did not share their experience. In other words, the mythological and the existential-historical were related in a way that makes ultimate distinction between them impossible.

Bultmann's desire to separate the two arises from his objection to the line of thinking which tries to argue from the mythological to the existential-historical—the line which would contend that the fact of there being something unusual about the happenings, considered in an objective-historical way, proves that

---

[37]*Kerygma and Myth*, p. 12. *Jesus Christ and Mythology*, pp. 32–4. Anders Nygren, "Christ and the Forces of Destruction", *Scottish Journal of Theology*, vol. IV (1951), pp. 363–75, and Alan Richardson, "Gnosis and Revelation in the Bible and Contemporary Thought", *ibid.*, vol. IX (1956), pp. 31–45, say this too, but neither uses the term "myth" in quite the same way as Bultmann.

[38]It would be more accurate to say, as far as the actual documents of the New Testament are concerned, that they arose because the readers for whom they were intended had already entered such an experience. But this would not be so in the case of most of the preaching described in those documents.

they may serve as the basis for, or are themselves, the events of redemption, and also from his conviction that, since the mythological does not prove the existential-historical, there is no point in retaining it.[39]

Actually, Bultmann at this point makes the same mistake as those whom he is attacking:[40] that of trying to separate what cannot be separated. Bultmann wants to separate them because he thinks that the mythological is a hindrance to the existential-historical, and those whom he is attacking want to separate them because they think that the mythological is understandable and convincing without the existential-historical. The point we are making is, as against Bultmann, that any person's experience of the existential-historical involves him inevitably in acceptance of what is mythological, and as against his opponents that if a person is not enjoying experience of the existential-historical no amount of arguing on the mythological plane is sufficient to bring him to it. On both sides there is a failure to appreciate that an ultimate separation of the mythological and the existential-historical is not possible.

[39] cf. Ian Henderson, *Myth in the New Testament*, p. 48.
[40] A similar instance is referred to by Ronald W. Hepburn. Bultmann, he writes, "is as anxious to *escape* the level of the verifiable as the logical positivists were to remain within it, making verifiability the touchstone of meaningfulness. Both are guilty through excess of zeal: the positivists in their belief that any simple verification procedure could prove adequate to every possible experience, Bultmann in refusing to make plain what states of affairs would be incompatible with Christian belief, or just how different the world would have to be before belief would have to be declared senseless." "Demythologizing and the Problem of Validity", *New Essays in Philosophical Theology*, p. 234.

Assessment

This consideration of an important contemporary position has confirmed us in our own. In being immediately related to Jesus the believer has to do with the Jesus whom he knows as a figure in history. In recognizing Jesus' uniqueness the believer is not adding to the picture of Jesus facts which have no relationship to the event but is establishing facts which, contributed to by what the historian himself is, constitute the most adequate interpretation of the data possible. These data cannot be labelled separately as "objective-historical" and "existential-historical", as if there could be two resulting pictures, one labelled "objective" and one "subjective", or "historical" and "superhistorical", or "universally true" and "true for certain people". For each historian there is one picture of the historical Jesus, and that picture is a fact which continually becomes a datum to be used in the establishment of a new fact—and always a fact which calls for a decision.

V

Conclusion

THE WAY BY WHICH we have travelled can now be reviewed.

It began by our noting the way in which the problem of Jesus looms large on the horizon of thought today, arising because of the place he has in history, where he stands as both like and unlike other men.

It has been suggested that his reality as a historical person can be considered at only those points where he is like other men and that whatever may be unique about him is beyond the sphere in which the historian works. There has emerged alternatively the suggestion that what he is as a historical person has no relevance for what Christians regard as the most important thing about him. Some have gone so far as to suggest that what he was as a historical person gives the lie to this importance.

All such suggestions put the Christian in a quandary. How can he continue to regard the coming of Jesus as highly significant if that event is not to be appreciated according to the usual canons of historiography? To have this question resolved is a constant need. The relationship between the figure known and open to historiographical investigation and the figure acknowledged by Christians as the supreme revelation of God is, we saw, the core of the problem of Jesus.

With this appreciation of the position as a starting-point we proceeded in chapter I to look at views of Jesus held during the last hundred years, and saw that these raised questions of considerable consequence for our own problem. What has been said over this period makes it plain that, to deserve serious consideration by historiographers, a picture of the historical Jesus must satisfy at least four conditions.

It must be evident in such a picture, first, that the historian has recognized that the four Gospels are neither a single homogeneous product nor a group of four independent witnesses. They are interrelated in a peculiarly involved fashion, and each part of what they say has to be considered in a manner appropriate to itself. One does not ask the same questions at every point, and one does not have the alternative of accepting the Gospels in their entirety or not at all. Each historian is free to accept some parts and reject others and each historian is bound to show not only that he recognizes this as the appropriate methodology but also that his own procedures of acceptance and rejection have been carried forward in a responsible manner.

A second requirement for a noteworthy picture is that account be taken of what critical scholarship has uncovered concerning the Gospels.

From the long and sometimes acrimonious discussion characterizing a century of New Testament scholarship the following have emerged as conclusions beyond question: that the Gospels do not always present incidents and sayings in the same context, that they disagree concerning some details of content, and that the writers have made use of earlier traditions and documents. Each of these points has been argued at length and in detail, but each now receives so large a measure of support that to disregard them in any serious attempt to find the historical Jesus is unthinkable. The development of these findings was the particular contribution of liberal thinkers who, applying to the Gospels the criteria used in scholarly investigation of other literature, showed that the espousal of critical methods and conclusions does not mean the end of Christian discipleship.

Our consideration of the "Christ-myth" view disclosed that there is a great deal of evidence to show that Jesus actually existed but little or none to supplement what is said of him in the four Gospels. It is to these primary sources therefore that the historian must refer continually, and even those who consider that the Gospels give a minimum of authentic information about Jesus himself are bound to show that they have considered their contents seriously.

Any picture of the historical Jesus presented for the serious consideration of historiographers must show, thirdly, that account has been taken of the circumstances in which the Gospels were produced.

It is important for the historian to keep in mind that the background of the Gospels is first-century Palestine. This was brought home sharply to European scholars of the twentieth century by Albert Schweitzer whose thought is variously considered to have spelled the end of liberalism and to have set it on a new and fruitful course. Certainly, since he wrote his best-known book it has been much less easy for historians to interpret Jesus according to criteria drawn from their own culture.

No less important is it to recognize that the Gospels took their rise within that Christian community and were influenced by it in their form as well as in their content. No Form critic's attempt to identify the *Sitz im Leben* of each pericope was ever accorded unanimous acceptance but, since the rise of the *Formgeschichtliche Schule,* no one disputes the assertion that the circumstance of communal motivation (if not communal composition) must be kept in mind.

Our survey of views in chapter I showed, fourthly, that any picture of the historical Jesus must have regard for factors to which the general currents of modern thought are not readily amenable.[1]

One factor which comes to mind immediately is the "otherwordly" element in the thought of Jesus to which Albert Schweitzer gave so much attention. As we saw, he gave it rather too much attention, presenting it in a distorted fashion, and it was left to C. H. Dodd and others to present it in a more understandable way. It cannot however be disregarded.

Another factor is that complex of features to which we referred under the heading of the uniqueness of Jesus. Within the Gospels there is little to define the nature of this uniqueness (that was left to the Fathers who built upon some essays which are discernible in the Epistles) but the Gospels point to ways in which it expressed itself.

The strangeness of such concepts to the minds of many at the present time makes it difficult for some historians to give them place in their picture of the historical Jesus. But no one who has considered the

[1]By "the general currents of modern thought" we mean particularly the attitude towards "science" to which we gave some attention in chapter II, pp. 84-94.

work already done in this direction can agree to their being discounted altogether.

These are the conditions which, it has been apparent for a number of years, must be met in every attempt to present the historical Jesus in a manner commendable to historiographers. It was the recognition of this fact which led us, at the end of chapter 1, to offer a tentative assessment. We cannot disregard whatever in the Gospels is incompatible with our own reconstruction of the life of Jesus, and we cannot look on the Gospels as having their only basis in the needs of the primitive Christian community.

This assessment, like every other, rests upon the work which New Testament scholars have done over the last hundred years or so, and which they are continuing to do. Their researches have made ours a time when the problem of the historical Jesus is opened up more adequately than ever before. McCaughey writes:

> Methods of literary criticism, of sources and forms of the tradition, knowledge of Palestinian conditions and language, awareness of the religious and perhaps particularly the eschatological perspectives of contemporary Judaism, all make possible a movement back from the situation in the life of the Church (which so often colours the Gospel records) towards a probable situation in the ministry of Jesus, a movement much more exactly *controlled* than was available a generation ago.[2]

---

[2] J. D. McCaughey, "The Question of the Historical Jesus", *The Reformed Theological Review*, vol. xx (1961), p. 7. He adds: "It is extremely easy however to use the greater knowledge to cheat and confuse."

To appreciate all this however is not to solve the problem with which we set out. Indeed an appreciation of what has been achieved in the field of New Testament scholarship only serves to underline the fact that the problem of the historical Jesus is one inherent in the New Testament itself. The material covered in chapter I made plain the need for a clearer understanding of what is meant when we speak of anything as "historical".

This led us to consider in chapter II the nature of knowledge of the past, for it is apparent that factors other than the statements of the Gospels themselves are brought into consideration by all who read them. We saw that all knowledge of the past involves the interplay of data and interpretation and that action by the historian himself is as proper as it is inevitable. There is an objective event but each historian establishes facts of his own. Although differences between historians would disappear if each one's facts could be thoroughly conformed to the event, the only possible way for their differences to be resolved is for them to engage in discussion of the data and interpretation each sees as relevant. None can compel another to conclusions which contradict his own facts, and it is no solution to declare out of hand that certain data are inadmissible or certain interpreations dishonest or foolish.

Thus the assumption that it is the picture of Jesus established by the unbeliever (or the believer in so far as he bows to criteria advanced by the unbeliever) which is historical is seen to be mistaken. The picture established by the believer can claim to be at least equally historical.

But to leave the matter there would be to deal with

only part of our problem and we therefore turned, in chapter III, to consider what it is that occasions the difference between the pictures of the believing and the unbelieving historian. We identified this as an immediacy of relationship, distinguished from others by the uniqueness of the one to whom the historian is related.

Three things may be said here about the uniqueness of Jesus.

The first is that the uniqueness of Jesus is a real event of the past. The Christian historian is confident that the facts he establishes on this score are properly related to what Jesus actually was. They do not arise only from the historian's apprehension of Jesus' significance for himself.

Christians have always manifested concern for the true humanity of Jesus and have done so for various reasons, chiefly dogmatic ones. We can see now that the true humanity of Jesus is of great moment for historiographical considerations. It is as a man in history that he shows himself unique, and it is thus that he is seen by the historian. This uniqueness of a person truly human is what enables the historian to say of him that he is divine. If it is objected that to be divine is to be beyond history, or to be something that no historian has the capacity to recognize, the reply is that such a line of argument would make it impossible for us to recognize any action on the part of God or indeed to say anything about him at all. At an early stage of our discussion we showed that one does not need to know everything about the event in order to judge whether a particular fact is true.[3] Similarly, the historian does not need to know all about divinity

[3] *supra*, p. 19

or uniqueness in order to appreciate that a certain event of the past is divine or unique.

The second thing to be said about the uniqueness of Jesus is that it does not depend on any relationship other than his own relationship to God. We spoke of this earlier[4] as the determinative aspect of his uniqueness, and we may recall here Knox's words. "The 'divinity' was not half his nature or a second nature, but was that purpose and activity of God which made the event . . . the saving event it was. The divinity of Jesus was the deed of God. The uniqueness of Jesus was the absolute uniqueness of what God did in him."[5]

From such an understanding of the historical Jesus there flow the classical dogmatic formulations concerning him.[6] He may be referred to as "the Word Incarnate", as "the Son of God" and as "of one substance with the Father" because he was, as a historical event, the manifestation in human terms of what God is eternally. We have no way of knowing all that this involves and may indeed regard it as presumptuous to enquire.[7] We do not even need to ask in what way he may have been conscious of his own uniqueness.[8] But we are bound to acknowledge

[4]*supra*, pp. 134-5.

[5]John Knox, *The Death of Christ* (New York: Abingdon Press, 1958), p. 123. cf. *supra*, p. 135

[6]The same thing is to be said concerning other concepts which have been used to describe his significance. Certain of these were discussed *supra*, pp. 123-33.

[7]cf. *supra*, p. 134-5.

[8]That is to say we do not need to ask this in connection with the matter being discussed here; in other circumstances of course it may be a very important question. I should myself answer it by saying that Jesus was conscious of filling a unique place in God's plans and had a corresponding sense of communion and mission. The dogmatic formulations as to his divinity had to

that his uniqueness arises from Jesus' relationship to God.

In the third place, the uniqueness of Jesus is known only by the historian who stands to him in a relationship of immediacy.

It is, as we saw, this relationship which enables the historian to establish facts of the greatest significance concerning Jesus, and the Christian historian is confident that his facts do not mislead him concerning the character of the event itself. We went so far as to suggest that there is an essential minimum of knowledge the absence of which would preclude discernment of Jesus' uniqueness.[9] That is to say, there are facts the failure to establish which deprives the historian of knowing what is most important about the event.

The Christian maintains that this is the truth concerning Jesus, and he cannot but aver that those who deny it have established facts which are false.

We went on to say that to recognize Jesus' uniqueness is an act of faith. This led us to consider what part faith plays in the historiographical process and to draw out the fact that integral as it is to the sort of person the believing historian is, its part is a quite legitimate one.

This legitimate part is always one in close relationship to the individual's historical knowledge. Faith cannot give to facts a guarantee which historiography denies them. What faith does is to join with other factors in the situation in enabling the historian to establish

---

await later reflection on the sequence of events which included some occurring after his death.
[9]*supra*, pp. 160-1.

facts which, in as thorough an interpretation as possible of as many data as possible, he sees to be sound.

As faith does not operate out of relationship to other existents, no more does it arise or continue in isolation. We therefore included in chapter III consideration of the way in which any individual's faith is made what it is because of activities on the part of the Christian Church and of God himself.

Finally, in chapter IV, we looked at our subject in the light of what has emerged in the controversy concerning demythologizing. There is no doubt that the putting forward of Bultmann's programme has raised in an acute way questions to which we have addressed ourselves throughout this dissertation: What is the event upon which Christian faith rests? In what sense is it historical? How does the Christian come to knowledge of it?

Both in their manner of posing questions and their suggested answers the demythologizers have done much to make Christians aware that the problem of the historical Jesus is very much a fundamental and presently urgent one. We can be grateful for this, and for the light that consideration of their position has shed upon our own.

This consideration did not however bring about any alteration of the conclusions we had reached in earlier chapters. Rather did it result in confirmation of what had been maintained there.

Historiographical enquiry is neither harmful nor irrelevant to Christian faith. It is on the contrary an activity as valuable as it is unavoidable, and the picture of Jesus held by the Christian, which is to some extent made what it is by the part which the Christian's peculiar relationship to Jesus plays in establishing it, can lay just claim to being a picture of what Jesus actually was.

Christianity is a historical religion. It really is through the man Jesus that God has been pleased to reveal himself, and to know more of Jesus is to know more of him who sent him.

Acknowledgements

Index

Acknowledgements

The author and publishers wish to thank the following for permission to use quotations: S.P.C.K.: *Kerygma and Myth* edited by H. W. Bartsch; T. & T. Clark: *Church Dogmatics* by Karl Barth; Edinburgh University Press: *History and Eschatology* by Rudolf Bultmann; The Open Court Publishing Co.: *The Meaning of Human History* by Morris Cohen; Clarendon Press: *The Idea of History* by R. G. Collingwood; Faber & Faber: *The Sense of History; Secular and Sacred* by M. C. D'Arcy; S.C.M. Press: *Demythologizing and History* by Friedrich Gogarten; Hodder & Stoughton: *Criticism and Faith* by John Knox; Oliver & Boyd: *The Christian Doctrine of History* by John McIntyre; A. & C. Black and The Macmillan Company, New York: *The Quest of the Historical Jesus* by A. Schweitzer.

GENERAL